PRAISE FOR THE WAY OF A BOY

"Simply told, this memoir of war, family, and endurance is a work of literature."
—1993 Drummer-General's Award Citation

"I was absolutely hooked by page three … The warmth and appeal of *The Way of a Boy* is obvious, but it is the clear, honest voice of the narrator that has the most penetrating impact."—Mordecai Richler

"A captivating read … As storytelling it is faultless, as witness it is undeniable … A very moving book."—Neil Bissoondath

"*The Way of a Boy* moves one by the gentleness, the considered truth, the simplicity that hindsight can bring. It is a very moving, clear-eyed view of atrocity beyond comprehension as seen through the eyes of an innocent. There is not a word too many, not a grief too small."
—Sir Dirk Bogarde

"A meticulous and astonishingly vivid recreation of one child's journey from a kind of paradise—life among the white-skinned 'plantocracy' of Dutch-ruled Java—into a kind of hell … At times sad, yet never the least bit sentimental … So powerful … the words … sting your eyes. A superlative book."—*The Globe and Mail*

"Hillen's style takes on an intensity that is quietly mesmerizing ... Hillen writes with such effective skill and achieves such a quiet poignancy that he goes right to the human, central experience of war's malevolence."—*Books in Canada*

"A moving, sobering, hope-filled chronicle of a nightmare that was real ... Hillen has shown that out of suffering, peace of mind can come ... It is a wonderful work with wide appeal. Those who read it will not forget it."—*Quill & Quire*

"Poignant ... If there is redemption by art, then the past is redeemed by this beautiful book ... an exhilarating read, radiant with the magic of far away ... Written in prose as clear and heady as good vodka, it summons up the lost years with a quiet irony that achieves humour as often as pathos."—*Toronto Star*

"Splendid ... The skill of the writing gives it a rare power ... What makes it so moving is its testimony that even the most degraded lives can (sometimes) be saved by the bonds of humanity. Such a book could not be written in anger but only in hope."—*NOW* magazine

"Courage, stamina, friendship, love, and some humour travel throughout this story of a family in wartime. And they mostly override the ghastly injustice, cruelty, brutality, anger, terror, and fear that also crowd the pages ... Totally absorbing ... It should be part of high-school and university English classes."—*The StarPhoenix* (Saskatoon)

"[Hillen's] account of what they ... endured so calmly, so without hysteria, and so without complaint, is to me something which is essential if the record of the immense suffering imposed by the Japanese in Southeast Asia is to be complete."—Sir Laurens van der Post

"A remarkable memoir ... modest and gentle ... [Hillen's] recollections, fifty years on, of his wartime internment by the Japanese must be far sharper than most people's sense of their immediate present, as if the pain and horror of the events he witnessed are still so vivid that they rush in an instant across half a century and stand quivering beside him."—J.G. Ballard, *The Daily Telegraph*

"What makes Hillen's account so poignant are the shrewd, knowing observations of a little boy, clearly recollected by the man he later became ... This is a moving, beautifully written, and totally absorbing account."—*Sunday Times*

"[Hillen] writes of the struggle for life, of hunger and disease, heat, brutality, smells, degradation, death, fear, with the simple directness and honesty of a child."—*Liverpool Daily Post and Echo*

"Startling ... magic ... a lovely tribute without a false note."
—Peter Worthington, *Toronto Sun*

"*The Way of a Boy* radiates humanity and deserves to become a classic of its kind."—*Ottawa Citizen*

"With Hillen the power of story-telling derives as much from what is left out as from what is put in ... A stunning piece of literature."
—*The Gazette* (Montreal)

"A magnificent, poignant recollection ... lyrical and evocative, as much an assault on the senses as equatorial Asia itself."
—*The Financial Post*

"A graceful and moving memoir ... More than a record of unusual events, it shows how, in matters of survival, the courageous refusal to abandon the heart's allegiances can make all the difference."
—*Maclean's*

"Ultimately, *The Way of a Boy* is as much about the gamut of human choice even in extremity as it is about the specific, and powerful, detail of Ernest Hillen's reminiscence."—*The Independent*

"*The Way of a Boy* is moving and true; the writer has bestowed upon those he remembers, dead or alive, a gift. And that gift is available to all who read this book."—*Australian Book Review*

"The reader is left in awe of the bravery, endurance, and solidarity of which humans are capable, as well as the brutality, evil, and divisiveness they can inflict."—*South China Morning Post*

"Moving and horrifying as they are, sometimes unbearably so, the gentleness and innocent freshness of these recollections are what stays in the mind ... Entrancing."—*The Sunday Telegraph*

PENGUIN CANADA

THE WAY OF A BOY

ERNEST HILLEN was born in Holland and moved to Indonesia when he was three. During the Second World War, he spent three and half years in Japanese prison camps in Java. He immigrated to Canada in 1952, where he has written for and edited a variety of Canadian magazines, including *Maclean's*, *Weekend Magazine*, and *Saturday Night*. He is also the author of *Small Mercies: A Boy after War*.

THE WAY

A MEMOIR OF JAVA

OF A BOY

Ernest Hillen

PENGUIN
CANADA

PENGUIN CANADA

Published by the Penguin Group

Penguin Group (Canada), 90 Eglinton Avenue East, Suite 700, Toronto, Ontario,
Canada M4P 2Y3 (a division of Pearson Canada Inc.)

Penguin Group (USA) Inc., 375 Hudson Street, New York, New York 10014, U.S.A.
Penguin Books Ltd, 80 Strand, London WC2R 0RL, England
Penguin Ireland, 25 St Stephen's Green, Dublin 2, Ireland
(a division of Penguin Books Ltd)
Penguin Group (Australia), 250 Camberwell Road, Camberwell, Victoria 3124, Australia
(a division of Pearson Australia Group Pty Ltd)
Penguin Books India Pvt Ltd, 11 Community Centre, Panchsheel Park,
New Delhi – 110 017, India
Penguin Group (NZ), 67 Apollo Drive, Rosedale, North Shore 0632, New Zealand
(a division of Pearson New Zealand Ltd)
Penguin Books (South Africa) (Pty) Ltd, 24 Sturdee Avenue, Rosebank,
Johannesburg 2196, South Africa

Penguin Books Ltd, Registered Offices: 80 Strand, London WC2R 0RL, England

First published in a Viking Canada hardcover by Penguin Group (Canada),
a division of Pearson Canada Inc., 1993
Published in Penguin Canada paperback by Penguin Group (Canada),
a division of Pearson Canada Inc., 1994
Published in this edition, 2008

1 2 3 4 5 6 7 8 9 10 (WEB)

Manufactured in Canada.

LIBRARY AND ARCHIVES CANADA CATALOGUING IN PUBLICATION

Hillen, Ernest, 1934–
The way of a boy : a memoir of Java / Ernest Hillen.

ISBN 978-0-14-316851-5

1. Hillen, Ernest, 1934–. 2. Prisioners of war—Indonesia—Java—Biography.
3. World War, 1939–1945—Prisoners and prisons, Japanese. 4. World War, 1939–
1945—Concentration camps—Indonesia—Java. 5. World War, 1939–1945—Personal
narratives, Dutch. I. Title.

D805.I5H55 2008   940.53'175982092   C2008-902134-7

Visit the Penguin Group (Canada) website at **www.penguin.ca**

Special and corporate bulk purchase rates available; please see **www.penguin.ca/
corporatesales** or call 1-800-810-3104, ext. 477 or 474

To Anna Cadwallader Watson Hillen

CONTENTS

INTRODUCTION by Charlotte Gray

In February 1942, a few weeks after the successful attack on Pearl Harbor, Japan invaded Indonesia. The Imperial government in Tokyo was eager to secure the Dutch colony's rich resources to fuel its war machine in Asia. In little more than a month, the invaders had overrun the archipelago, putting an abrupt end to over three hundred years of Dutch rule. A whole colonial way of life, centred on government offices, tea plantations and army parade grounds, suddenly collapsed. Between 200,000 and 250,000 Dutch men, women, and children were packed into hastily built and overcrowded internment camps. Month after month, the internees struggled to survive while rations shrank, conditions deteriorated, and the Japanese guards grew increasingly cruel.

By the time the Japanese surrendered to Allied Forces three and a half years later, about one-fifth of those internees had perished. The Indonesians themselves fared even worse at the hands of the invaders: during these years, famine and forced labour killed millions of the archipelago's citizens. For Indonesians, the Japanese occupation was a watershed in their own history. Once the war was over, their country moved rapidly towards independence. In contrast, Dutch internees limped and staggered out of prison camps into a land where they were no longer welcome. They had to swallow both the traumas of their camp experiences and the disappearance of their world.

In the immediate post-war years, the hardships faced by Dutch internees in far-away Indonesia rapidly faded from memory, overshadowed by the horrors faced by Jews within Europe. By the time the internees were repatriated to Holland, their Dutch relatives had little interest in their suffering.

However, half a century after the Japanese invasion of Indonesia, a slim memoir entitled *The Way of a Boy* by a Canadian writer captured the internees' experience for a new audience. Ernest Hillen was three when his Dutch father and Canadian mother moved from Holland to the mountains of Java, where John Hillen took a job on a tea plantation. The idyllic life of swimming pools and saronged servants came to a crashing halt when Ernest was eight. That was the year the soldiers came, first for his father, and then for his mother, Anna, Ernest, and his older brother, Jerry. By the time Ernest was eleven, he had seen prison guards beat up defenceless women, watched his best friend die, and lost all hope that there would ever be an end to the war.

The Way of a Boy quickly became a bestseller, largely thanks to word of mouth. Ernest had achieved something magical: he had reinhabited his boyhood self as he told the story of his wartime experiences. The brutalities, terror, fear, and horrific injustice are described in unsparing prose, yet the story radiates the directness of a child. There is grace and unexpected humour. Young Ernest's innocence, shot through with hope and quiet poignancy, captivated reviewers in North America, Europe, and Australia. "I was absolutely hooked by page three," wrote the late Mordecai Richler. "The warmth and appeal of *The Way of a Boy* is obvious, but it is the clear, honest voice of the narrator that has the most penetrating impact."

I had known Ernest Hillen's voice for several years before this book was published in 1993—in fact, I knew the voice before I knew him. In 1988, we both worked for *Saturday Night* magazine: I wrote a column about national politics from my home in Ottawa, and he was my editor. Each month, I would send my copy to the magazine's editorial offices in Toronto, and a few days later my phone would ring. "Hello," I would hear, noting a certain deliberation in the soft voice—a deliberation that suggested my caller's English, although now thoroughly mastered, was not his first language.

The voice had qualities that I grew to love. Unlike many editors, Ernest never tried to rewrite the column in his own clear, quiet style. He might say, "There's just a teeny little point here where I think you might ..." Or, "I wonder if you've got exactly the right word here ..." There was a hesitancy—but alongside the hesitancy, there was a perceptive intelligence. Ernest knew when, for whatever reason, something didn't ring entirely true.

Each month, our faceless friendship grew—and the phone calls got longer. After a few minutes of editorial discussion, we would move on to discuss homes, children, books. The voice became clearer. Every now and then, there would be a great burst of laughter or a wonderful exclamation—*"Godverdommen!"* (Dutch for "goddammit")—that sounded as though Ernest was clearing his throat. And, as Ernest recounted anecdotes from his own life, I learned that the voice was the vehicle for a magnificent storyteller. His stories took time, because there were so many significant details—the background traffic sounds, the size of the restaurant steak, the wolfish smile on a man's face. And his stories had shape, because he had thought about them as he himself tried to make sense of an event and find the significance below the surface. I would listen, mesmerized.

Occasionally he would interrupt himself to say, "Are you still there?"

When Ernest and I finally met, in the magazine's Toronto office, we didn't know what to say to each other. It was an editorial meeting, I remember, and there were several people there—busy, self-assured, trading jokes, jockeying for position at the editor's table. At first I hardly noticed the stocky man with a watchful expression and a shock of dark hair flecked with grey who slipped quietly into the room and sat at the far end, closest to the door. After a few minutes, someone addressed a remark to "Ernest," and I turned in surprise to him. He mumbled a reply, his brown eyes hidden behind heavy-framed glasses. Then, when everybody else's attention had moved elsewhere, he lifted his head and gave me a wonderful, warm, mischievous smile.

Over the next few years, our long-distance friendship blossomed. Yet I discovered little about Ernest. He confided that he wished he had had more education, yet never mentioned that (as I subsequently learned) he had less than five years of school. He told me that he had lived in Indonesia, but only relentless questioning prompted him to mention he had been in a Japanese internment camp during the Second World War. I was impressed with his career: he had written plays for the CBC and been a senior writer and editor with major publications. But he always downplayed his professional achievements. "It was just a little thing," he would say. "It wasn't that big a deal."

When he began to write *The Way of a Boy*, he was equally self-deprecating. "It's just a little book," he would explain. Over the years, a handful of short articles describing his experiences in the camp had been published, and I wanted to know more. Growing up in England, I had been surrounded by people scarred by the war—a cousin whose dad had been killed, an uncle traumatized by three years in a prisoner-of-war camp, an aunt struggling to raise her son on an army widow's pension. Yet somehow, their tragedies were remote ordeals. Their stories were sad, but they didn't touch the heart in the way that Ernest's did.

Why did Ernest's tale of those years in the Japanese camps have such an impact when it was first published? Because of that voice. It is, of course, not entirely the same voice as I heard on the telephone from the disembodied editor in Toronto. The voice in *The Way of a Boy* belongs to a wide-eyed child, not a middle-aged magazine writer. Yet the voices share the same simplicity, thoughtfulness, and ingenuousness. Ernest's memoir is saturated with the same attention to detail as I used to hear on the phone. The smokey smell of Manang, the gardener. The taste of hard-boiled egg. The sound of women crying quietly in the barracks. And there is the same search for shape—of the story, the meaning, what it reveals about human nature.

The reviewers were not the only individuals captivated by Ernest's memoir. First a trickle, then a flood of mail arrived at the Penguin offices in Toronto after the book appeared. Many of the letters came from people who had also been in prison camps during the Second World War (and not necessarily in Indonesia). Many of those individuals had never spoken about their experiences. Now, Ernest's simple account of what it felt to *be* there and go through all those grim times allowed them to explore their own memories. In 1995, *The Way of a Boy* became the first personal account of internment in a Japanese prison camp to be published in Japanese. It has now been published as a book in four languages and in condensed form as an article in *Reader's Digest* magazine in at least a dozen countries.

When *The Way of a Boy* first appeared, many of Ernest's friends were astonished by the precision with which the author recalled the details of his extraordinary childhood. This was no journal of events vaguely remembered then embroidered with literary flourishes and invented dialogue. Nor was it all-the-facts journalism, dressed up with trappings of the novel. I recognized that his memoirs were permeated with what he always pushed me to achieve in my columns—the ring of truth. This author had looked down the dark tunnel of years and summoned back into his mind incidents and personalities that glowed with almost tangible authenticity. Then he had transformed them into polished literature. "How did you *do* that, Ernest?" I asked. "How did you recreate that world so that I, as your reader, could explore alongside that small boy the smell, touch, and feel of an alien world?"

"It was hard," he told me. He had never brooded about his years in the camps, so there was no pent-up angst, no residue of anger, to be released once he had begun. There were the stories his mother still told about his childhood—but Anna (as the book makes clear) faced fear and hardship with caution and good sense rather than a burning sense of injustice. Once the war was over, her message to her two sons was always: "We survived. Let's get on with the next damn adventure." Prison camp experiences had not become the defining motif of Ernest's life.

Instead, Ernest was propelled towards writing the memoir by his urge to write. When he started the project, he had plenty of enthusiasm for the project, but little sense of direction—and, in his words, "a very ordinary memory." There were only wispy threads of recollection, and he wasn't sure what would happen if he pulled at those threads. Would they, like fishing lines, catch deeper memories, lurking in the opaque waters of his psyche?

Ernest was convinced that every individual's memory is like a ramshackle and uncatalogued warehouse, bursting with every experience its owner has had. The requirements for accessing the warehouse's contents, he believed, were time and tenacity. "I needed a splinter, a trace, a shadow of something no matter how dimly recalled—a sound, a smell, a snippet of sunburned skin, anything really," he explains. "Then I would bombard that bit with questions. A torrent of uncensored questions coming at great speed, unarticulated, of every imaginable kind, on and on, lambasting that smidgen of information. After a while it would seem that my mind was boiling, but I knew that if I just kept up that barrage long enough a bit more would come swimming to the surface. Soon, I would have two specks of something. And the barrage of questions never slowed until there were three specks of something, and so on. And then suddenly, magically, there might be a full sensation or a complete image. Rain drumming on a roof, the smell of dried sweat, a long-forgotten face."

A single image was only one piece of the puzzle: Ernest was looking for the whole jigsaw. "Am I in that rain or watching it from a dry place? And why? Is it my dried sweat or another person's? And where am I? And whose face is that? The avalanche of questions swells and swells because there's now ever more there to probe. On and on. Sometimes there's even a flash as clear as a movie. Only fatigue … slows the interrogation, and it comes to a stop."

It was an extraordinarily intense period for the author. Sometimes he would disappear alone to his cottage near

Bracebridge, Ontario, where there was just him, his laptop, and the water pump. There, the process of mining his psyche could be so powerful that he would lose all sense of place and time. Occasionally, he would resurface, shaking and breathless, to discover a whole day had passed. The experience was akin to psychoanalysis without an analyst in the room, checking his watch. Sometimes, Ernest admitted, he found himself weeping. The tears were prompted, he says, by "remembered grief or fear or anger, or the instances of courage and kindness and, above all, grace that I had witnessed once." But the journey back in time was also a triumph in itself, so the tears were not always about the past. "I cried from the sheer exhilaration of having excavated those memories, of having made them mine." And that is when the writing would begin—slowly, word after word, like a poet.

At the time that Ernest was writing *The Way of a Boy*, my own three sons were still young. I recognized that Ernest had truly captured the mindset of small boys—their curiosity, energy, sweetness, and relentless egocentricity. Young Ernest assumed that his mother's main job was to look after him and Jerry, and his trust in her ability to do so was (with the exception of only one occasion) absolutely unassailable. But every now and then as I read *The Way of a Boy*, I would lift my eyes from the page and wonder how his mother coped. While Ernest was totally absorbed in the here and now, finding ways to amuse himself, she knew the danger they were in. While her younger son stole lead or threw stones, she watched Japanese guards behave with incredible brutality. Anna's courage and good sense insulated her son from the stress she felt—and allowed him to behave in the way of any boy. The title he chose for his first memoir is perfect.

THE WAY
OF A BOY

ONE / The Plantation

SOMETHING MAKING soft sounds underneath the plank floor woke me. Very quietly, so as not to rouse Jerry next door, I climbed out of bed and pressed my ear to the boards—and heard breathing. It would be completely black down there now. Even during the day it was a dark place because of the spider webs that hung from the edges of the small raised house; to wriggle underneath I had to lift the webs aside with a stick. But I liked crawling around in the cool sand, especially after midday when the sun turned white and banana trees lost their shade.

The breathing was coming in slurps. It was looking for something to eat, of course, but nothing lived there; I'd never even seen a snake. The little house, called the "pavilion" for some reason, stood behind our main house on the plantation. Jerry and I had our own bedrooms and in front was a long room lined with so many windows it got boiling hot during the day if the shutters were left open. Lying underneath the pavilion, I knew just where everything was—Jerry's bed, my bed, the cabin trunk holding my harmonica wrapped in a white handkerchief, and my iron collection. Down there, I sometimes listened to Jerry, who was eleven, and our mother doing his lessons; he correcting her Dutch because he spoke it better. And I lay there in the shadows when Jerry was punished, usually for lying, and locked in with the shutters closed so he couldn't even read. I would tell him stories through the floor; he was four years older so I don't know if he liked them but there was nothing else he could do. Some of the stories were about a Chinese girl who roamed in high red boots over hills and through valleys. She had adventures and because she liked to stop and pick unripe mangoes to eat with salt she often had diarrhea.

With my ear still to the plank floor, I heard a snort then and knew what was beneath me—a wild boar. I'd never seen one because they live so deep in the jungle, but Manang, our gardener, said that they were as fast as locomotives and sometimes went crazy and would run you down and rip you to pieces. If they strayed onto the plantation, usually at night, they could hurt young tea bushes or people, and they had to be killed. Lately, Mr Otten had shot three of them. Mr Otten, the plantation's mechanic, was the only white man left; the other eight, my father too, all Dutch, had been taken away by Japanese soldiers in a truck a few weeks earlier. This had happened on all the plantations. It was 1942; there was a war on and, for now, the Japanese had won. We were living in the mountains on the island of Java in the Dutch East Indies (Indonesia). Mr Otten was a short, kind, half Dutch, half-Indonesian man with a tiny moustache who had been allowed to stay behind to take care of the factory, and to keep his rifle. He hunted the wild boars together with Indonesians carrying spears with real steel points. Whenever Jerry and I asked if we could come along on a hunt Mr Otten said "Absolutely!" but never kept his word; Manang cut bamboo spears for us anyway, just in case.

I lay unmoving on the floor and it snorted again. I wasn't scared: it didn't sound mad. Imagine having one as a pet! Another snort, and a grunt, but not so close now; it was wandering away. With great speed and terrible strength I threw my

spear into the boar's side—no, into its eye—and black-red
blood spurted out. I climbed back into bed.

Manang smelled of different kinds of smoke. He never hurried
and I liked being near him: it was restful. My father and the
other men used to return from the tea gardens in shirts dark
with sweat, their faces wet. Not Manang. He never looked hot.
Manang wore faded khaki shorts that used to be my father's, no
shirt, and a straw hat that hid his eyes. His large flat feet had
spaces between the toes because he didn't have to wear shoes.
I had felt the bottoms of those feet and they were hard and covered with deep, dry, criss-cross cuts which he said didn't hurt.
I wanted feet like that, and his shiny brown skin, and I tried to
walk bow-legged like him. Manang usually worked squatting,
slowly moving along in the quiet warm air like a duck. That's
how he chopped at the lawn with a long knife, that's how he
weeded or dug or planted. That's how, from bamboo and from a
certain soft wood, he would carve guns, knives, arrows, whatever
we needed; we had only to ask. And that's how, from half peanut
shells, splinters of wood, and bits of banana leaf, he built boats
to sail on a puddle; you lay on your stomach and blew the boat
from shore to shore. Manang almost never seemed to need to
stand. He didn't often say much, and I don't know if he had a
wife or children or where he lived, but he let me stay near him.
    When it rained, Manang would squat on the edge of the
covered walkway behind the house along which were ranged
the tool shed, kitchen, bathroom, and garage; he would smoke
the thin cigarettes he rolled and watch the rain, watch it from the
distance racing nearer, watch it shake the bushes and drench
the grass. He could wait, he had time. When the sun was out
you could see far across the hills that glimmered in every shade

of green, and the clouds moved high in the sky. But in the drumming, clattering rain the world grew small. Manang stared ahead, smoking, not moving. It was safe near him. There were others like Manang, old men who couldn't work any more, who stayed up all night around the plantation, cigarettes glowing in the dark, guarding us whites, our homes, our trucks, the tea factory. It was good to know they were out there, smoking, watching.

But it has to be said that Manang was not brave; at least he had some cowardly spirits inside him. He himself had told me about spirits—spirits inside people and animals, in the air, on mountains, and in trees where during storms the souls of children cried. Spirits everywhere, and clearly some that could undo Manang. Jerry and I sometimes built war planes from upside-down garden chairs and invited "the girls," who were visible only to us, into our cockpits and made calm, joking remarks as we turned loops and strafed enemy soldiers. That was brave.

And Jerry was brave after our father left. Our father had a bull terrier called Leo, white with brown spots, who listened to no one but him. If the dog didn't obey quickly he'd be shouted at or slapped; if he did, there was no praise because, of course, he was behaving as he should. This, my father said, was how Leo learned "discipline"; Jerry and I were taught discipline as well. When my father was home it was safe to unchain the dog and let him run around and Manang would feed him. But after the soldiers took my father away, Leo wasn't set free at all—and it drove him wild. If he saw someone, anyone, he ran forward so fast his chain jerked him upright and there he danced, snarling and barking. Manang was not brave, because once my father was gone, he never went near Leo again.

It was Jerry who pushed water and food to the angry dog with a broom—and afterwards sometimes vomited. I, of course, was too little to do it, and Jerry would have stopped our mother. This was probably because of what our father had said to us on the day he left. He said it while the truck holding the other white men waited with the motor running and soldiers stood on guard, the bayonets on their long rifles glittering in the sun. He had shaken Jerry's hand and then mine and let his blue-grey eyes burn into our brown ones. His dark blond hair was combed flat back, freeing his forehead and highlighting his eyes. They could see inside your head. If you did something wrong he would shoot you his look, even when there were visitors. It was foolish to lie to him; Jerry tried and nearly always tripped up. On that last day, standing on the stone front steps, our father had said to us, slowly: "Take care of your mother." Well, maybe Jerry knew what he meant, but I had no idea. It was a strange thing to say. How could a little kid take care of his mom? Make her laugh? Bring her tea? It didn't make sense. She was there to take care of *me*.

That day we had been told at breakfast that our father was going down the mountains to a "camp" for men only. Our parents talked in tight voices, in English so we wouldn't understand. My father needed all my mother's attention; they hardly noticed us. There was tea and porridge and we could have one slice of bread with sweetened condensed milk. For months we had watched adults listening to the radio, chewing their lips, smoking a lot. We had heard bombs fall far away and seen planes painted with the red ball fly over. Sitting at the table, we understood that it was a serious time—a camp was really a jail; our father didn't know where it was or how long he'd be there. Since dawn he'd been packing and repacking the one suitcase he could take. During those moments, as our parents prepared for parting, Jerry and I cleaned out the can of condensed milk.

When Manang pretended Leo didn't exist, my mother told him this had to stop, that my father was counting on him. Manang agreed, asked forgiveness, and avoided the dog. And then Leo broke loose—and Manang slipped away. My mother and Jerry and I escaped into the house, and the cook, who in her tight sarong would squat over the coal fire on the kitchen floor, locked herself in along with the washerwoman. Leo trotted back and forth in front of the beds of pink and red oleanders beneath the windows, watching for a face to show; if he saw one of us he'd stand very still and bare his teeth. We were prisoners. Left alone with two children and a mad dog, our mother, her face a little pale under her freckles, told us Leo was Daddy's dog, Daddy loved him, and Daddy wouldn't want him hurt. Thirty-five years old, slim and straight, she paced the living room, her long fingers touching a vase, a tablecloth, her swept-up dark red hair; I always thought her hands moved like a queen's. Her serious brown eyes stared out over the waves of tea bushes broken only by patches of jungle. A decision was needed. What would Daddy do? she asked. It wasn't like her at all. She was proud of her "common sense," inherited, she said, from Grandpa Watson, her father in Canada. "Maybe I'm not as smart as so-and-so," she might say to my father, "but I've got more common sense." Finally, though, she phoned Mr Otten to come with his rifle. She told us that Mr Otten had wondered how he could get a good shot with Leo on the loose. How could he even get out of his car?

Without saying a word, my brother Jerry got a tin of corned beef from the dining-room cupboard where dry goods were kept, opened it with its little key, and shook out the beef. Clutching the fatty meat, he ran out the back door to the tool shed calling, "Leo! Leo!" The dog came storming around the corner just as Jerry pulled open the shed door. He held up the corned beef for Leo to see and threw it inside, but before Leo dove after it he bit Jerry's hand. Then Jerry slammed the door shut.

That was brave action by Jerry, and unusual: what he really liked was to be alone and read. Sometimes he would sit in the front pavilion room late at night and read by moonlight. He almost never yelled, grabbed things away, or beat me up, although he could have because I liked fighting and he was stronger; he didn't enjoy fighting though. Sometimes he teased, but not for long. And when we played, I forgot he was older. Jerry was caught lying—and then got it with my father's thin leather slipper on his bare bum and was locked up for whole days in his room—because he couldn't keep his eyes steady; he never learned to hide what was inside him very well. He wasn't quick to smile, so that by the time he did, it often didn't seem sincere.

One day when I was about four and we were alone at home playing cowboys and Indians, which Jerry knew about from books, he shot me in the eye with a bamboo arrow. The eyelid had shut in time and as I jumped and yelled the arrow was swinging from the eyelid without harm. What Jerry did was just pull the arrow out, sit me on a sofa, put his arm around me, and read out loud from one of his books without pictures until I fell asleep. That's how our parents found us when they came home from playing bridge; the eyelid showed only a tiny red mark. On the evening before I turned seven, after I'd gone to bed, he was allowed to work through the night cleaning his bicycle and then painting it pale grey; he wrapped the saddle in blue ribbon. It was my big present of the day; sitting on the crossbar

I could just reach the pedals. It had to be the finest thing Jerry owned but I wasn't so surprised when he gave it to me.

Mr Otten was phoned back and when he drove up it had begun to rain hard. From inside the house the three of us watched him march to the tool shed, part a bunch of strands in the bamboo matting of the door, and stick the rifle through. The gun jumped twice.

Jerry and I took off our shirts and in our short pants we went out and dug the dog's grave by the purple bougainvillaea near the front-door steps where our father had said goodbye. It was always okay for us to be out in that warm rain; our mother watched from a window and let us be. Water half covered Leo after we lowered him into the hole: he really wasn't very big. Mr Otten had shot him in the head and in the throat but the rain had washed the little holes clean. We shovelled the wet red earth on him, stamped and slid about on the grave to flatten it, found some rocks and pressed them in on top. Looking down with clasped hands we said things we thought our father might have said to Leo and we cried; then we thought of more things to say so we could cry more. Manang didn't come back that day.

The morning after the snorting under the floor I went to see Mrs Plomp. The houses on the plantation were near each other and I enjoyed making short visits, to tell a story or to hear one. Mrs Plomp was the youngest woman and the most beautiful. All around us in villages and hamlets tucked away in the bush lived thousands of Indonesians, unhurried people with dark eyes, liking laughter, loving children, kindly but able to turn suddenly *mateklap*, mad with anger. The women in their tight sarongs walked with tiny, swaying steps, never a hair out of place. Most of the people worked in the tea gardens and the factory, a few in our homes. At night through the trees you could see points of light from their oil lamps; they had no electricity. I knew many and visited them in their smoky, dark, bamboo huts where often a picture of Queen Wilhelmina in a huge dress with wide shoulders hung on the wall. They were poor, ate with their fingers, didn't speak Dutch, and I never saw one in the swimming pool except to clean it. So Mrs Plomp was the youngest, most beautiful, *white* woman. She had long red nails, thin arms, and blonde hair that trembled on her neck.

Once I had knocked on their door and Mr Plomp, a big man, also blond, had answered, his face as red as a beet. He told me softly to come around another time. I ran home—they lived across the road from us on a hill of grass and flowers—and my mother told me that Mr Plomp that morning had received a telegram from Holland saying his father had died. After Mr Plomp was picked up by the soldiers with the truck, Mrs Plomp would wander around her house in short pants and shirts that were much too big for her; the pantlegs and the spaces between the shirt buttons were so wide I could see her underwear. Maybe they were Mr Plomp's clothes and she wore them because she missed him.

On top of a high carved cupboard in Mrs Plomp's dining room stood a glass jar filled with red candies. As soon as I spotted it, I didn't look at it again. I told Mrs Plomp that food was important, and she agreed. I said that to stay healthy you should always try to eat healthy. I asked her what were the things she enjoyed eating most, and she named some. Then I mentioned a few of mine: fried bananas, soup with *balletjes,* cucumbers, red candy, peanut butter, fruit salad. "Red candy?" Mrs Plomp said, astonished. "Look!" she pointed to the jar.

When I told Mrs Plomp what I'd heard the night before under the floor her eyes widened and she shivered—and I don't think she was pretending. Her house was very near ours; she lived alone and I was, after all, talking about a real live wild boar poking around in the night. I was sure that's what I'd heard. Mean, hairy, dangerous things with big teeth curling up out of their mouths. Killers. At breakfast I had mentioned the spurting blood and Jerry and my mother had stayed calm. After she gave me my red candy, Mrs Plomp said that perhaps I should warn Mr Otten. I was happy she believed me, and I promised I would—after swimming.

Every morning, before lunch, all the white families strolled up to the swimming pool. It was the choice spot on the plantation: from it you could see all our houses, the soccer field, the factory, the main road. On weekends we took picnic baskets and spent almost entire days there. Jerry and I had few toys, but every day held the certainty of play in the pool. It was never denied (except to Jerry on lock-up days). On birthdays we were allowed to jump in with our clothes on. If it rained, my mother said that was all the more reason to go. In bed I planned amazing jumps and tricks for the next day.

With the men gone, except for Mr Otten, it wasn't as much fun at the pool. The men knew how to be rough and throw kids around. There were cabins to change in for girls and women and for boys and men. The walls were made of the bamboo matting, *bilik*, and it wasn't hard to pull a few strands aside and peek through. Jerry said he once saw two breasts but couldn't tell whose they were.

I liked the water. Whatever fear I might have had I lost when my father picked me up one day, carried me to a corner of the deep end and told me to make it across that corner where he would wait for me—and dropped me in. I was about four. Scary, yes, but it also meant that while I thrashed towards him he was interested in me. And when my father was interested his attention was total. With his hands he could make or repair or draw anything; he read a lot and seemed to know everything in the world. It felt wonderful inside his attention. In a book he showed us pictures of the gloomy-looking men whose music he turned up loud; pianos, violins, flutes; some pieces he could whistle from start to finish. A few times he let us listen to his gramophone records. We had to sit still and terrible itches would begin; Jerry and I never looked at each other—one giggle and you were out. Lessons in discipline, but we didn't mind. We watched the little beige lizards called *tjik-tjaks* flit about the walls after insects. Manang once cut the tail off one to show it didn't bleed and that the tail went on wiggling by itself; he promised that a new tail always grew back on. My father listened to his music with eyes staring or closed, frowning, humming, dipping and shaking his head. When it ended he would say *that* was music, the *only* music. We were happy to have been near him.

I wasn't five yet when I dog-paddled the pool's length, eyes wide open beneath the surface lit by the sun. When I came up for air adults clapped their hands. A year later I made the length under water back and forth. Even the best swimmer on the plantation, Mr Witte, the chief administrator, had a hard time doing that, and would burst up out of the water gasping. Mr Witte, who was mostly bald, had a deep voice, and powerful, hairy forearms. He laughed a lot and hard, and let no one forget who was boss; even at picnics he gave orders. His wife wasn't like that. Mrs Witte was a small woman, erect and proud, polite even to children. She wore yellow and pink starched dresses and she limped a little because one leg was shorter than the other and a high shoe held its foot. In a bathing suit, barefoot, she had to hop, but then she'd dive into the pool and smoothly breast-stroke lap after lap, eyes ahead, chin up, never wetting her hair. Mr Witte's eyes followed her into the water then followed other women, walking, sitting, easing themselves into the pool; my mother, too, when she took off her bathing cap and her long red hair fell loose. Some women felt his eyes and glanced up and then his eyes would lock on theirs until they looked away. I saw this—everybody did. Chief administrators were kings on their plantations, I heard my father say once. I think he liked Mr Witte, liked his discipline.

I went to see Mr Otten at work after lunch. The factory hummed and puffed out the dry smell of tea; inside, machines shuddered and roared. Everywhere on the plantation it was quiet, the littlest sound carried and hung. Wind breathed on leaves, on high grass; for long moments it was utterly silent. It was only in the factory that you couldn't hear the birds or thunder. Mr Otten wore oily overalls left unbuttoned to the crotch to keep cool. He was now the only boss and very busy but he too believed me about the boar and said he would send a man to check its tracks. As usual he said "Absolutely" when I asked if Jerry and I could come along on the hunt. When I argued that this boar was a little bit mine, Mr Otten stroked his moustache but didn't answer. So I asked if I might go look in his machine shop if I didn't touch the tools, and he let me.

Everywhere I walked in that time it was with my eyes to the ground—scanning for nuts, bolts, nails, pieces of wire, anything metal. The cabin trunk in my bedroom already held a large-size Blue Band margarine can full of metal. I picked up bits around the plantation and when we had gone to the city,

Bandung, I had found lots in the streets. From the machine-shop floor I crammed steel filings into my pockets. No one knew why I collected metal. Jerry had asked, and so had my mother, and I'd said it was just something to do.

But I had lied. There was a huge plan. I dreamt about it. When I was three we had come to Indonesia from Holland on a marvellous steamship with one funnel. My goal was this: when I had enough metal I would melt it all down and then build just such a ship—except mine would have two funnels. More metal was needed, much more—it would take years—and meantime it was best to keep the scheme secret. Drawings I had made I pinned up in my room, but of course nobody knew they were of the plan. People would have laughed. For many months in the city and on the plantation, I carefully gathered small metal things and stored them in the cabin trunk. I had patience; lots of it. One day everybody's mouth would fall open.

Everybody also meant Ineke and Hanneke, their baby brother Erik, and their mother and father, *Tante* Ina and *Oom* Fred Staal—"aunt" and "uncle" because they were our parents' best friends. Uncle Fred was the administrator on another, a rubber, plantation some distance away; Ineke was Jerry's age, Hanneke about two years older than I. There were no schools in the mountains so for more than a year our two families had rented a house down in Bandung; when school was on, the mothers took turns every other month staying up at the plantations with their husbands and looking after the kids in the city. Aunt Ina, like my father, was much sterner than my mother, or Uncle Fred; she could be fussy and was hardly interested in my stories. I had known Ineke and Hanneke since I was three. They were like sisters; all four of us had brown eyes. Ineke wore long pigtails and when I was younger she let me use them as reins;

Hanneke allowed me to keep some of the lifelike horses and dogs she drew. Mostly, though, Jerry and I were on our own, had only each other to play with. Sometimes we joined Indonesian kids on the soccer field and kicked around a coconut husk tied together with string; nobody owned a real ball.

One morning a few days after I had seen him at the factory, Mr Otten drove up to our house in a small truck and when he shut off the motor he called my name. From the back of the truck he and a helper lifted something heavy wrapped in a sack. I came running up and Mr Otten whipped back the cloth. There was the cut-off head of a wild boar covered in black-red blood and flies. He had shot it the night before and was sure this was the animal I had heard under the floor. Its small yellowish eyes stared up at me. Mr Otten said he hadn't been able to take me on the hunt but here was the head. A present. If I buried it in the ground and let worms eat the hairy skin and the meat, they would leave a beautiful, clean, white, wild boar's skull to put in my room. The boar had roamed around in my mind a lot and for a moment I felt sorry it was dead—but I could *see* the clean white skull.

Jerry and I got shovels and dragged the head up into the garden which rose behind the house. Manang grew sweet potatoes there, and peas, beans, papayas, and pineapples. We began to dig in an open space among the pineapples. It was the spot where we smoked and from which we could see the road on which our father drove home on his motorcycle. We stole his American cigarettes, not often, from a little latched cupboard in the living room that also held Bols gin, cheese biscuits from our Dutch grandmother just for him, and playing cards; in the evenings adults played bridge a lot at each other's houses. One day our father came home on foot and must have seen the smoke from the road. When we noticed him he was already running. We threw the cigarettes into the sharp pineapple leaves and started running ourselves. I looked back to see if my father was gaining, and he was, but smiling a little, so I just let myself drop, and Jerry did too. His back to the sun, our father towered over us, a black giant with legs spread and hands on his hips. Even though we couldn't read his face, we rolled on the ground, kicking and laughing. No punishment that time; he only made us promise to stop smoking because it was bad for us, and we knew that.

Jerry and I looked for Manang to help us dig but he had made himself invisible. Dig deep, Mr Otten had warned, because in the heat the meat would quickly start to smell. He was right. Two days later in the afternoon we found the hole pawed open. Up close the stink from the rotting head already crawling with tiny white worms made our eyes water. We had to dig deeper. Jerry helped pull the thing out but then left me alone. I tied a teatowel over my nose and mouth, breathed in deeply as I did at the pool, ran to the hole, dug, then hurried away for fresh air. Back and forth, back and forth. It was the hottest time of day, very still, and it seemed hours passed with the hole hardly changing. My knees hurt; I cried. My mother watched from a window. Finally the hole was so deep I could stand up in it. I tumbled the head in, shovelled down the loose earth, and piled big rocks on top. Now I would wait.

Time passed, wheeling about on Jerry's bike, swimming and diving, searching for metal, sitting near Manang. When you woke up most mornings everything was hidden in mist; then the burning sun would slowly undress bushes, trees, houses, and the rolling green hills stretching as far as you could see. The quiet on the plantation sometimes made you drowsy and you lay down in the grass below whispering leaves. We listened to tree frogs whistling and the swelling and fading of cricket song. Jerry and I had our hair cut very short in a chair on the lawn by a village *tukang tjukur*, barber, who also massaged our heads, tapping sharply with his fingers until we felt it down to our feet and almost fainted. We boxed wearing Jerry's thick socks from Holland on our fists—and somehow I always won. Through high grass sharp as knives we chased snakes. One slid into a hole and Jerry yanked it out by the tail: that was brave. And with our spears, we hunted down many wild boars and panthers. We pretended to be horses, like the Indonesians did on their New Year's, when they ran around on the soccer field with glassy eyes eating grass and bucking. That was a great feast, alive with spirits. Everybody dressed in new or carefully ironed sarongs and blouses and shirts; they prepared huge meals of roasted meat, fish, spiced rice, and fried bananas; they put on shadow-puppet shows; on a dozen differently shaped gongs they played music that long after hummed on inside you; they danced, telling long, old stories of battles, love, demons, and wicked kings where every slow twist and turn, even of a little finger, had meaning.

The days wore on, with meals, usually Indonesian food, at a certain hour, bedtime always the same; my mother sat alone then and wrote letters to family in Canada and Holland. In the afternoon heat, I still sometimes sat beside her as she rested on her bed, brushed her long hair and told Chinese-girl adventures until she fell asleep; I had done it often when I was small. And every day at four tea was served with a biscuit—a must, no exceptions; my mother said she wouldn't "be herself" without it. First, though, Jerry and I had to splash water on our bodies with a bucket from a bricked-in tub in the bathroom so we could drink tea "fresh and clean." Calm days, safe days. Then one night at supper our mother said quietly, "Boys, I have some-thing to tell you." And our world changed.

She began, "This is serious ..." and in the times to follow she would never need to say that again: we would know. She brushed us with her fingertips, looking from one face to the other, and took a little breath. "Tomorrow it's our turn to go on a truck," she said. "The Japanese are coming to pick up all the women and children. They'll be here early. We're going to a camp, like Daddy." Then she smiled, "And I've got presents for us!" She brought out three new backpacks made of khaki cloth by a tailor in the village, the smallest one for me. Besides mattresses, the Japanese had said we could take what we could carry, she explained; so a rucksack and a suitcase each. Jerry and I could stay up late and make piles on our beds of what we wanted to take; later she'd come and check it out and add mosquito nets, towels, bed linen, and so on. Should she pack knives and spoons and forks? Soap? Medicine? She talked to us, I noticed, as if she really wanted to know what we thought. We should concentrate on clothes, she said, and use our common sense. And as she would now often say, "This is an adventure, boys."

It was long past our bedtime when she came to the pavilion. Jerry had to put back most of the books he wanted to take. I had lifted the margarine can with iron stuff onto my bed. "Ernest, little love," she said, eyes soft, putting her hands on either side of my face, "that's too heavy." She said I could take my little har-monica wrapped in the white handkerchief. It was a present from my father on my sixth birthday; I could play a bit from "Silent Night, Holy Night" on it.

She wasn't a mother who touched a lot. She sat down on my bed and pulled me on her lap, and Jerry came and leaned against her. "This'll be over one day, you know," she said.

"Nobody knows how long we'll be, or even where we're going, and we have to leave everything behind, but one day this'll be over." Her hands stroked us, our hair, our arms. She rocked herself a little bit. Looking at us but not really talking to us she dreamily said things in English that we didn't understand, but we didn't mind. Outside a bird shrieked in grief; spirits sat very still in the dark trees and probably on the roof. That was all right. We were her children and the night wouldn't harm us. It was the last time, I think, that I didn't feel at all grown-up.

TWO / Bloemenkamp

ALL OF US HAD TO STAND in the back of the two old open trucks bumping and jolting out of the plantation next day. The soldiers with the rifles had yelled and pushed—*Lekas! Lekas!* meaning "Hurry! Hurry!," one of the few words they knew in Indonesian—until all the white women and children from the area plus their baggage and mattresses were crowded on; they should have brought three trucks. The drive down from the mountains lasted many hours and it got hotter and hotter; no breeze reached me. Pressed together we swayed around corners and didn't speak because the jarring could make you bite your tongue. The sides of our truck hid everything from me except the sun, sometimes the crown of a bowing coconut tree, and the cloud of red dust from the truck ahead.

Halfway through the day we stopped in a village for water for the radiators, not for us; no food either. We were told to stay on the trucks. I stood on a suitcase to see over the side. The soldiers had jumped to the ground and were yelling orders at the villagers. I needed to pee and my nose and mouth were full of sand. Across the road I saw a girl sitting on a low whitewashed stone wall by a holy banyan tree. She wore a brown and gold sarong knotted under an armpit and her long black hair hung loose and wet; she must have just had a bath. She was twelve or thirteen years old, a woman already, and looked so cool and clean and rested. She watched the shouting soldiers and the heads of the white women sticking up out of the trucks, their hair wild from the wind. And then her eyes met mine—and a warmth went through me that I hadn't felt before. I looked and looked and wanted terribly to go to her. She was pulling me to herself. Her mouth once moved a little; it could have been a smile or maybe she said a word. Then the truck jerked forward and we were off again. For many months I kept her inside me: she would flare up in my mind and I would feel that warmth and miss her. She had looked so free.

It was the hottest time of day and my mother shoved our backpacks together so I could lie down; Jerry and she went on standing. We were going to a camp in Bandung one of the soldiers had told a woman who spoke a little Japanese. I shut my eyes against the sun. There were swimming pools and soccer fields in Bandung, there was a restaurant that offered many kinds of ice cream, and on the sidewalks Indonesians cooked spicy food wrapped in banana leaf for one cent a portion. Jerry and I used to buy it whenever we had a cent; it was forbidden, of course, because it might be dirty and give you diarrhea. There were good hilly streets in Bandung for roller-skating; my father had promised I would get roller skates one day. My father had been away six weeks already—how long would we be gone? In a month the boar's head would be clean and white and beautiful. Would Ineke and Hanneke be in the camp? In Bandung there was plenty of metal stuff on the streets, but it would be too heavy to lug around. Would somebody steal my margarine can?

When I couldn't hold any longer I peed in my pants on the rucksacks. I could smell the dried sweat on the silent women bouncing above me.

After the long ride down from the mountains, the soldiers stopped the trucks outside Bandung at a girls school because the camp wasn't ready yet. The classrooms had broken windows and were full of flies. In some corners there were brown messes on the floor; people must have been locked in because the school did have outside toilets. Desks lay scattered about the yard in high grass. The air was much warmer than on the plantation. The guards, none of whom was taller than the tired, sweaty women, at once began barking orders. I would almost never hear the Japanese simply speaking, not even to each other. Their strange words exploded out of their mouths in short bursts and hit you, they heated your skin, and made you feel your heart thud. The soldiers stomped around, restless, angry, their small black eyes showing nothing.

They shouted at the woman who understood a bit of Japanese. She said she was told, first, that we were stupid and lazy, and then that we must clean the floors of two of the rooms and carry in our mattresses from the trucks. She said she had asked for food but was told no, maybe tomorrow. When our three mattresses were down, two next to each other and one across at the end, my mother went outside with a tin cup. She came back with small yellow flowers in the cup, laid down a suitcase in the centre of the mattresses and set the cup on it— we had a table. The other suitcases and the backpacks she placed around us on the edges of the mattresses—and we had our own room.

Darkness came suddenly, as happens in hot countries. There was no electricity but some women had brought candles. The air hung thick, our shadows dragged along the walls, we whispered. For hundreds and hundreds of nights, this was how it would be: people, strangers, all around you. Then we heard voices outside, Indonesian women's singsong voices and the guards' harsh ones. The women's voices, soft and sweet and warm, were begging, begging to see us, please, the white women and their poor little children. There was a soldier's grunt—and they flitted in, barefoot, sarongs rustling, carrying baskets and pots wrapped in cloth with roasted meat, fish, soup, rice, fruit, tea. The smells breezed ahead. They knelt down among us, serving, giggling and clucking and moaning, urging us to eat, to eat more. Oh these were bad times, and Allah knew it. Fragrant brown women with tiny quick hands and tight buns of black hair glinting in the candlelight. They had seen us arrive from their village, and they knew there was no food. Eat more, please.

We were there a few days and the women fed us. Then trucks came that drove us into Bandung, into our first camp, a section of the city that had been closed off by an eight-foot-high fence of plaited and split bamboo rimmed with barbed wire. It was called Bloemenkamp, which means Camp of Flowers. Its single gate was guarded day and night by soldiers who would let you through only if you were extremely sick or dead. In time, Bloemenkamp held five thousand women and children. We didn't know it was to be just our first camp; adults were certain the Japanese would lose the war soon. There were always rumours of Japanese defeats and victories for our side. Far away, cool and calm American pilots dropped bombs with a smile. The rumours came from hidden radios and from women who read the future in the cards.

With five other families we were crammed into a bungalow on a short street with a church; the only furniture in the house was an upright piano in the hallway. Mrs Witte and her daughter Mieke lived there, too. I believe Mieke, who was thirteen, and her older brother, Piet, who had been picked up with the men, had paid little attention to us on the plantation because their father was chief administrator. That was probably also why Mrs Witte and Mieke moved into the front room with the big windows. Soon it wouldn't matter who you had been; no one would care. The three of us got a small storage room without a window, in the back.

Once the mattresses were down, my mother went out for flowers. Wherever we lived there would be flowers, or leafy twigs at least, in cups or jars or bottles. From an old magazine she cut pictures and let us pin them up; she draped a shawl across two nails already in the door. With twine she hung a sheet across the room: we slept on one side, she slept on the other, always staying up late reading by a light bulb shaded with black cloth. She was reading *How Green Was My Valley*. In the beginning she and Jerry were able to get hold of books, which would later be forbidden. The last book she would have was called *The Hermit*, about a wise old Swedish man who lived on a mountain and gave advice to people. My mother liked it so much she copied it entirely, late at night in tiny writing in an old exercise book, until that, too, was confiscated. Her side of the room was also the "living room" and where we ate. We settled on her bed and she told us, keeping her voice low, that to get through this time all we needed were three things: shelter, food, and hygiene. Well, here we were in our room, the camp had a communal kitchen, and there was good pressure in the water taps.

Dirk stood watching us from the sidewalk the first day. About my age, he wore dark blue short pants, a starched white shirt, and socks and shoes. He had black hair and blue eyes, wasn't tanned, and spat often. He had a smart way of tossing back his hair which kept falling forward. His father, now in a men's camp, had been pastor of the church down the street. We would become friends, for a while, and, as I tended to do with some people, I aped him a bit. Not in dress. That was his mother's doing; the socks and shoes were just silly. But I was soon flipping my head back, too, although my hair was short as a brush. And I began to spit.

There was a small split between my two upper front teeth and with a mouthful of water I could spit a fine long squirt; but mostly I relied on saliva. I spat and I spat, left and right and in the air, at a fly, a tree, a smudge on a wall. If I missed I spat again—the target had to be hit. Dirk's spitting was a habit; mine was something I felt I could learn to do better, like swimming. I practised when I was alone outside, and inside, sitting on the toilet. One day my mother and two other women were visiting Mrs Witte in the front room and I was on the sidewalk spitting steadily. The women watched through the big window and laughed. Mrs Witte did feel though that she had to mention the traces of spit on the bathroom walls and ceiling. My mother didn't order me to stop all spitting, just to quit it in the bathroom.

What I liked especially about Dirk were his lead soldiers. He had a shoebox full of them, standing, kneeling, lying down, all shooting, all in Dutch uniform. He let me play with them but I was usually the Japanese or Germans and he was the Americans, British, or Dutch. He also had first choice of troops and picked the battleground, his yard—he and his mother had to share their home next to the church with other families, but, as Dirk said, it was still his house and his furniture. Sometimes he would choose my yard because our garden had a patch of plain earth good for digging tunnels and trenches and, after a rain, building forts.

Dirk and I were alone a lot because, of course, there was no school of any kind, and adults and older children were at work.

Prisoners had to run the camp: keep it clean, the above-ground sewers too, cook the food, take care of the sick. We new arrivals were told this by the camp's commandant on the second day, standing at attention on a soccer field. We had waited for him in the sun for two hours with babies crying, people fainting, and not even children or old women allowed to sit down. There would be many such waits in the camps on fields in the sun. When he and some of his staff marched up, I noticed officers wore neat, brownish uniforms as compared with the scruffy, yellowish ones of ordinary soldiers; few of any rank, though, seemed to have footwear that fit. Their dragging feet made a special "sloff-sloff" sound which, walking bowlegged as they did, I tried out for a little while.

From the belt around the commandant's big belly dangled a curved sword and his riding boots gleamed in the sun. He had a tiny moustache like Mr Otten's and stood yelling at us from a three-foot-high wooden platform without steps. He had jumped onto the stand without a run-up, like a cat. I was amazed. Weeks later, at another meeting on the field, we watched him with the same quickness beat up a guard who had broken some rule. In a moment, hands and feet flying, he had the soldier curled up on the ground unconscious, his head a bleeding mess.

The commandant's translator, a young woman who was half-Indonesian, half-Dutch, had told us to bow to him at her order *Keirei!*—and from then on to bow to all Japanese soldiers. She showed us how: stand at attention, then bend your upper body forty-five degrees. You straightened up at the command *Naore!* She said the bowing was really for the Emperor of Japan and warned that an incorrect bow would be seen as an insult to him.

Arms across his chest, legs wide, the commandant shouted at us for a long time. He said we were very fortunate to be under the protection of the Japanese army; we would be told this often. In return we had to keep order, not try to escape, be thrifty with water and electricity, not cause fires, kill flies, keep clean and healthy, always dress decently, not gamble or drink— and practise self-discipline. We would be treated with respect but disobedience would be punished. "You must," he bellowed, "perform useful work in wartime—it's a moral obligation!"

Quietly our mother repeated and explained it all that evening in the "living room." "We will obey them," she said. "They are the strong ones. They have the guns." She pressed her lips together. "We're going to survive. So, don't ever be cheeky—and don't ever look them in the eye!" Then she made us stand up and hissed *Keirei!* Jerry and I bowed and she bowed back. We bowed and we bowed at each other until the three of us flopped down on her mattress laughing.

My mother was made a mover, hauling furniture out of houses and, after sorting—chairs, tables, beds, cupboards, even pianos, also clothes, kitchenware, and paintings—loading it onto huge wooden carts that had been pulled by buffalo before the war. These she and other "furniture ladies" then pushed to already emptied houses for storage for the Japanese: to be used in their quarters or shipped to Japan. She did this all day long in the sun, growing brown and thin. Jerry was put to work in the kitchen where boys his age lifted drums of boiling water or soup or rice from wood fires and toted them around on bamboo poles. I was left alone.

Toy soldiers were new to me. My father had disapproved of our owning any "on principle." He didn't mind Manang's pistols, rifles, knives, swords, spears, and bows and arrows; but soldiers no. What happened when I played with Dirk's soldiers was that they became real men for me, clever or disobedient or funny, some very brave. Long after the day's battles were done they went on in my head on my mattress, for thinking soldiers made unexpected moves. But my men weren't really mine. Dirk, finally, was general of both sides.

I needed soldiers of my own—suddenly more than anything else in the world. There was only my harmonica to trade but Dirk already owned one; he had a lot of toys. I told my mother that it was important that I get some soldiers fast, but she was no help. What then? Could I pray, I asked. We weren't a religious family; I had even heard my father say that the church was "nonsense." Still, once in a while on the plantation, when I was sad, maybe after I'd found some dead animal and buried it, my mother said I could pray if I wanted to. It wasn't hard: you put your hands together, closed your eyes, and talked to God inside your head. He knew who I was, she said. But my mother wasn't so sure about bothering Him about soldiers. She looked at me. "On the other hand," she said, "you've already got No—maybe you'll get Yes!"

I prayed for soldiers. I told God I wasn't asking for many, five, ten at most, and that I needed them to do battle with as real men who could be smart or stupid and talk to each other. With ten soldiers I could even play without Dirk. I thanked Him for listening.

A sort of answer came very quickly. If I wanted soldiers so badly, Dirk said next day, he knew how to get some. After dark we would climb on the roof of his father's church where sheets of lead held tiles together. The lead would still be soft from the sun and we could just peel pieces off. He knew somebody who had a mould for soldiers and would melt down the lead and let it cool and harden in the mould. Dirk said he'd filched lead before, even stuff from inside the church, though he didn't say what.

I thought about it. The answer was out of a fairy tale, so simple—but strange: God saying go ahead and steal from a church. It didn't sound like Him, yet it seemed a definite Yes. There was no one to talk it over with. I knew what my mother and brother would say.

That evening I asked if I could play at Dirk's house for a while. I'm not sure my mother liked him: I was always so quiet after our games; but she said yes. It was still behind the locked church and grass and weeds had grown high. Dirk had taken off his socks and shoes. A ladder lay against the wall and he certainly needed my help propping it up; once we were on the roof our bare feet stuck to the tiles and the lead came off like toffee. My unease faded away up there high in the night with bats whooshing by—spirits probably.

A day or so later Dirk told me, sorry, no soldiers; the owner of the mould had botched it. The melted lead had spilled or the mould had broken, whatever. He was impatient. Forget soldiers. He had spotted a papaya tree with several almost ripe fruits in the garden of a house where everybody worked during the day. We'd steal the papayas; maybe we'd get stomach-aches but it was worth it.

Dirk's soldier collection grew larger day by day. I couldn't tell the new ones because he had rubbed them in dirt. It was more fun playing with more soldiers, but they were his and so were the rules. I was angry and then I was sad. I watched Dirk, hair hiding his eyes, digging a trench. He already had lots of soldiers—but he had cheated a friend. What was wrong with him? And what about God's fast answer? It had been a definite No.

Finally I told my mother, not about the lead, just that I thought that Dirk wasn't always a good boy; he was what Indonesians called *pinter busuk*, smart-rotten. I said I felt bad and as a friend, shouldn't I be helping him? She didn't ask me to explain it more. She said the best way to help was just to stay myself. I should also make other friends though.

And just at that time my brother got me interested in something else entirely. Jerry had watched Manang make things, too, and now he said he was going to build me a kite. Somehow he had gathered bamboo sticks, yellow paper, glue, and string. Early on lots of homemade kites flew over the camp, then fewer and fewer, and finally none. Some were run with thread specially coated with glass dust that easily sawed through ordinary string—and then you watched your kite float down, finders keepers for the kite hunter who got to it first. There usually wasn't much point chasing it.

Many of those kiting with glass thread were boys who, like Mr Otten, were half-Dutch, half-Indonesian; just about everybody with European blood, except Germans and, for a while, Italians, was interned. Often from poorer homes, where even the youngest smoked right in front of their mothers, the Indo boys were small for their age, dark-eyed, unsmiling, thin, and quick as crickets. They loved to fight, especially white boys, using their hands and feet; some had even been taught jujitsu by older brothers. If you were bigger, that was more reason to take you on. They roamed the camps in small gangs—and they could smell fear. Often, out of the blue, one would come up, chest out, and push up against you yelling, "I dare you!" and keep at it, his friends goading him on. Talking didn't help: he wanted to fight. You could run but he was probably faster—and you didn't because it wasn't brave and, anyhow, they'd follow and wait in front of the house. The fight ended with the winner sitting on the loser's chest rolling his knees into the muscles of the loser's upper arms until he cried *Ampoen!* meaning "Mercy!" in Indonesian.

The threat of these fights never stopped. If Jerry and I were together we backed each other up, if necessary tackling one of the others in the group; but we were apart a lot. I liked fighting but hated it with those boys. While wrestling they'd rub the clusters of elastic bands they wore around their wrists against your face so it burned. They didn't bathe much and had *daki*, crusts of dried sweat and dirt, on their necks, under their arms, and behind their knees. But mainly I was scared, me, who wasn't afraid of a wild boar! Nearly always smaller, an Indo boy either whipped you—so you lost to a little kid; or, if being bigger you beat him, you were a bully and one of his friends took over— right then, or another day. Loser or bully, you couldn't win.

Yet in time, I have to say, I became friendly with some of them. This was because of my laugh. I had invented a new laugh, a hard, shrill whooping, not for use at home. It sounded wild, even crazy, and at first gave me a little shock: no one laughed like that. I did it out on the street alone for a while, practising. When I thought I had it right, I whooped as I passed people, strangers. I couldn't read their eyes but they noticed: it was a surprise. I tried it on Dirk and he gave me a quick look. Nothing funny needed to happen for me to laugh my laugh; I liked its being unexpected. One day I laughed near a group of Indo boys playing marbles. I was looking down so it didn't seem as if it was aimed at them. I did it again. Was it that the laugh and fear didn't match? I edged up and squatted and watched their game, and they let me, and I whooped again when I wandered away. I kept the laugh and carried it like a weapon through all the camps.

It took Jerry two evenings to put together the kite. I sat with him as if he was Manang. The kite was shaped like a diamond and when we let her up she caught the wind with a rattle and climbed way above the coconut tree in the yard next door. I promised myself that one dark night I would fly her over our house, which is how you chase off bad spirits.

To get the kite in the air alone—Dirk couldn't be bothered to help: it wasn't his kite—Jerry had shown me how to stick the bottom end of the middle spoke just deep enough into the ground so it wouldn't fall over, walk away a few steps letting out string, jerk lightly, and start running. On that cloudless day it took many sweating laps across the damn lawn with the damn thing wobbling behind refusing to catch the damn air. "Damn" was one of my mother's favourite English swear-words; the others were "hell" and "goddamnit." She muttered them right through her Dutch, which wasn't the best, making people smile. Damn is *verdommen* in Dutch and she used that, too. Anyhow, the damn kite finally took off and in a second scaled our roof. Giving all the line she wanted I sprinted around to the back yard. The space was small but less closed in by trees and wires. She was alive now and with a will of her own, and I was just a little friend on the ground. She looped and climbed as she wished. She raced to the left, streaked to the right. She soared higher and farther, a yellow flash in the blue. She was well beyond the wall of the camp—flying in freedom. If only people could see her!

Then from two streets away there rose a purple kite, slowly first, then climbing quickly—straight and with purpose towards mine. For a moment I didn't understand. Then I furiously started winding her in, but I was too late and too slow: my kite was far and the pull on the string so strong. The killer kite closed in without pity. It never needed to gain great height or make it past the wall. It was low and near to where I was standing when its evil, deadly line crossed mine, just a touch— and at once that yellow angel in the sky began to drift, swoop, and tumble, faster and faster, and then she was gone. But outside the wall.

The worst heat of the afternoon was over and I was walking down our street to meet my mother coming home from work. I had played alone all day, and eaten cold rice with peanut sauce by myself; besides Dirk, there weren't many children nearby. Later I would become a roamer and wander anywhere in a camp. Ahead I caught sight of Dirk and some kids I didn't know in the driveway of a house where no one lived. He and I had several times circled that house, trying doors and windows; inside hung paintings and big mirrors and the furniture was covered with sheets. Dirk said the owners had run away to Australia before the Japanese landed. The doors of the garage were wide open and the group was throwing stones inside.

Dirk was in charge. He said you could only pitch rocks, one at a time, from behind this line in the gravel—and drew it again with the heel of his shoe. He had somehow forced the garage's lock and in the back had discovered a steamer trunk. He had prodded it open and found it packed with frilly glassware, vases, bowls, all sorts of glasses. He showed how a wet finger run around its rim made a glass sing; the singing came from around you, not the glass itself. Bigger gravelstones lay all around the trunk. It seemed a shame to smash that lovely glass. Dirk said one of these days the movers, like my mother, would come and carry everything off for the Japs. Anyway, he said, he was pretty sure I couldn't hit the mark.

But I did, with my first stone, and heard the rinkling inside the trunk. The next few missed. You needed skill, just as with spearing boars and panthers. It wasn't strength but aiming with narrowed eyes. You lined up stone with trunk's centre, saw stone flying, saw it landing in trunk—and then you fired. I wasn't watching how the others made out; I didn't care.

Tired adults were coming down the street, the workday done; they kept on walking. Some older boys stopped and joined in, kindly staying behind Dirk's line.

And then, behind me, my mother's voice: "Stop it! All of you—get away! Go home! And Ernest, you come here!"

I was shocked. To yell at children, strangers, and chase them off. To get mad—in public. Other women did that. They screamed at their children, beat them, in front of everybody. Not my mother. If she was angry, she spoke to us, alone, scolded maybe, explained, and sometimes made laws.

She was silent on the fast walk home, and so was I. Once when we were visiting Aunt Ina—she and her children had also been brought to Bloemenkamp—several women talked about how to keep their children from growing wild. One had said she was now both mother and father and hit her children whenever they "asked for it"; kids understood force. Aunt Ina had told the others that Erik was very young, and Ineke and Hanneke were girls and no trouble. Another woman had admitted almost crying that she couldn't beat her daughter and son, couldn't and wouldn't. My mother had said she didn't hit us, didn't believe in it—although her husband did—except if we "insulted" her; but that hadn't happened.

In our room my mother drank a cup of water, and out of her mesh bag fished a *djeruk,* a small green orange, sweet and juicy inside. She first made a cut around the top and bottom, then stripped away the skin in between, and pulled off the round pieces last. It was a little operation I'd seen her do a thousand times. Her hands dealt with many tasks always in the same way;

it was restful watching her. She broke the orange in two and handed me the big part. This I expected as well.

"It's never going to happen again," she said, her voice low. "You touched—and broke—what belongs to someone else and that's stealing. You know what stealing is. Well, we are not thieves." Her eyes looked into mine. "And this place is not going to make us thieves. Think about what I'm saying. Understand me. We're not going to discuss it any more."

No scolding, just the law. I felt strange: I couldn't remember ever being angry with her before. But she had yelled in front of other people. She hadn't asked questions, or for my side of the story.

"You yelled," I said, trying to sound like her. "And that stuff is going to the Japs anyway."

She didn't reply. She was thinking. Looking nervous, she leaned forward, hesitated, then smacked my face with her open right hand. I was stunned: it hurt—but most of all because the slap had come from her. My father hit, not my mother.

"The Japanese have nothing to do with this, Ernest," she said quietly. "I told you to think about what I said, to under-stand me. And you don't talk like that to me: it's insulting." She looked away. She would slap me only once more, towards the end of those months and years—and then she would strike me with all her strength.

I put my mind to what she'd said and mostly understood it. Certainly I felt a little older. I played less and less with Dirk.

THREE / My Wound

IT'S HARD NOT TO THINK about food when you're hungry. All you can do to keep it out of your mind is to play or sleep.

There was enough to eat the first few weeks in Bloemenkamp. At the communal kitchen you stood in line with aluminum pans that fitted into each other for soup, rice, boiled vegetables, bread, chunky brown sugar, milk for babies, and now and then a piece of fruit, or an egg. For a short while there was a store in the camp, which was fine if you had money. But if you had very little money, like my mother, you bartered clothes or jewellery or whatever you had for extra food. You could also trade with Indonesians, at night, through, over, or underneath the bamboo camp wall. It was smuggling, *gedekken*, and the Japanese weren't strict about it—yet. They first just wanted everybody inside the camp and to have it running right.

But the rations grew smaller over the weeks, the months, and then the years. It happened so slowly you didn't notice until you remembered. Also, there suddenly might be a treat, more sugar, more fruit, or a day, or several days, when the helpings were "larger." Rumours flew then: the Japanese were losing badly, or winning, and having a change of heart—false rumours that never died. And people grew thinner.

Hunger makes you brood about food, dream about it, and, especially, talk about it. At least the women and older girls did, endlessly, about recipes and their preparation, though many, of course, had never cooked before the war; their servants did. I never thought about food on the plantation; it was there. I liked potatoes, when we had them, in thick gravy, green beans and parsley, fried chicken, fried fish, fried eggs, fried rice, fried bananas, tiny fried red onions, condensed milk, boiled tongue, ginger cookies, coconut cookies, buttered corn, shrimp chips, a sweet lemonade in which drifted what looked like frog-spawn— and fruit salad: from mangoes, oranges, papayas, bananas, melons, *rambutans, sawos,* and pineapples, sliced above a bowl on the kitchen floor by the cook squatting in her sarong, juice dripping from her fingers. What I didn't like was cheese; all I could think of shouting on the phone to my grandmother in Holland was, "I hate cheese, *Grootmoesje!"* In the camp, food was on my mind a lot and it made me impatient: it shouldn't have been so important.

Adults said we weren't getting enough protein, fats, and vitamins, that our nourishment was out of balance. This made your body weak: if you became ill, your body had little strength to fight—and there was almost no medicine. It was dangerous to get sick. My mother tried to prevent Jerry and me from catching diseases or hurting ourselves; herself, too. She minded herself as much as us. But she didn't go overboard. She used her famous common sense. Many mothers were too fussy and tight with their children, not letting them climb trees, play in the rain, fight, drink unboiled water, explore; their kids turned into soft scaredy-cats. Other mothers seemed tired, confused, frightened, and their children grew wild. They talked back to their mothers, hit them even, never helped, stayed up late. What my mother did was ask us every evening about our day, in detail, and when something came up that was dumb or unsafe we'd discuss it. Climbing trees was fine; going up a dead one, well, its branches snapped off easily and you could fall and break your arm or neck. She almost always talked to us as if we were adults and she was just the oldest and knew most: "Trust me," she said. "I want to trust you." But sometimes she lost her temper and her swear-words would fly. She had laws about bedtime, bathing, not staying in the sun too long, and so on. And she was stubborn about routines: always saying "Good-morning" at the start of the day; drinking tea in the afternoon (or hot water if there was no tea); talking in the evening; and celebrating—our birthdays, those of friends in the camp, my father's, those of family members in Canada and Holland and of the royals of both countries, and all feast days of both. "It's fun," she told us. "This is how we'll survive.

One way she took care of herself was to insist that certain times of every day were hers. There was her reading into the night if she had a book. And when she came home from work, sweaty and tired, she might ask us to get out for a while. "I have to be alone. That's how I restore myself," she would explain. "Take a little walk." It wasn't so bad being kicked out with Jerry. But when he was gone, she kept it up. I'd be waiting for her with stories, and she'd ask me to go away. "I'll listen to you better later," she would say; she would relent if I was sad or not feeling well. (Our mother also never shared with us her regular food ration as some mothers did who couldn't bear seeing their kids hungry. She said it wasn't wise to do so because the women risked illness and death—it happened often enough—and leaving their children orphans.)

The three of us talked while we ate the evening meal, usually thin vegetable soup and boiled rice, and we tried not to complain about the size of the portions. To get more food people grew it: tomatoes, spinach, sweet potatoes, carrots, onions, cabbages, lettuce, beans, hot peppers, herbs. The back yard was divided into five plots, one for each family. We guarded our crops because already people were stealing in the night. One stole in daylight—a guard nicknamed Johnny Tomato.

As Johnny Tomato patrolled the camp on his bicycle, he would keep his eye out for edible tomatoes. If he spotted a red one, he'd jump off his bike, pluck it, and eat it on the spot. It was foolish to let your tomatoes ripen on the plant. One day he snatched a tomato in the front yard of the house across the street. He saw me looking at him eating it, and I quickly straightened my shoulders and bowed from the waist as I was supposed to.

Johnny Tomato grinned at me and swung onto his bike—he liked kids. Most of the soldiers did, and if a child broke a rule he or she was seldom punished. They would find the mother.

I watched Johnny Tomato slowly ride down our street and then just before he reached the corner there was a woman who hadn't bowed quickly or deeply enough, or maybe he didn't like her face. Anyway, Johnny Tomato got off his bike and wheeled it yelling up to the woman who was still bowed and rammed the front wheel between her legs and hit her with the flat of his other hand, and then with the back of it, many times on the sides of her head, on her ears, until she crumpled onto the road. Then he climbed back on his bike and pedalled around the corner.

I ran over to where the woman lay. Two old women were helping her sit up. Her head was wobbling, blood dripped from the left ear, her eyes stared, not even crying.

I wanted to turn and walk away from the beatings I saw, but I couldn't: my neck was in some grip and my feet seemed nailed down. I sweated and watched. I saw every slap, punch, and kick, heard every yell, shriek, and cry. When Japanese rage erupted, the air quivered; strange anger, dark, their eyes giving no hint of it. Some roared and beat crazily. Some grunted and went at it with all their might. Some silently hit and kicked precisely to hurt, on and on. The women, or teenage girls, were rag dolls with no feelings, with no parts of their bodies special. They could moan and whimper and scream *Ampoen!* but that didn't stop the military men. Mercy was missing. They quit when their minds cleared, or they felt satisfied, or they were tired.

For forgetting to bow or bowing wrong I saw so many women and older children slapped and kicked, sometimes until they fell down, that after a while I didn't bother telling my mother about it any more. Because the thrashing by Johnny Tomato had happened on our street, I talked about it at home that evening. By the light from beneath the black cloth we could see each other's eyes shine. My mother listened; she was good at that. She nodded, thinking. From a worker on her team who had visited Japan, she said she had heard how Japanese men treated their own women; they were expected to obey and never to complain. For white women, the woman had said, Japanese men had even more contempt. They also despised prisoners. They themselves would rather die than be captured; honour meant more than life. So white women prisoners were like dirt and guarding them was shameful. Maybe that explained some of the anger and meanness, my mother said.

Then she spoke slowly, saying something she would say again so we would remember it. "They are your enemy," she told us. "They have guns and they are dangerous. They don't like you, even if they smile at you. They don't like any of us. We are their enemy and if we disobey them or get in their way they will kill us. Always be polite, always be serious, always stay calm. Don't laugh, don't smile, don't joke. Don't look them in the eye. You may lie if something in you tells you that you must. I am afraid and I know that you are afraid. But you'll be less afraid if you remember what I'm telling you."

Enemy, enemy—I'd never had an enemy before.

A part of our patch of garden, about as big as a dining-room table, was left empty for me to play in; that's where Dirk had come with his soldiers. The earth was often moist and good for building castles, forts, the decks of ships, and for digging secret tunnels. I had also buried a dead rat there so that, as with the boar's head, the worms could eat it and leave behind a clean, white, little skeleton.

One day, lying on my stomach scooping out a tunnel, I brought out my right hand full of earth and saw a drop of blood on the middle knuckle of my forefinger. It didn't hurt. Maybe there was a sliver of glass in the ground. I wiped the finger on my pants, but more blood seeped out. So I went to the kitchen and held it under the water tap and when the water washed away the dirt I could see a cut as tiny as an eyelash. I held my finger upright, the bleeding soon stopped, and I went back to digging.

That evening the joint was red and the edges where the skin was slit swollen. My mother cleaned the cut and made a bandage from a strip of bed sheet and wrapped it around the finger. She said it wasn't serious. "You've had lots of cuts." Most aches and pains didn't impress her much, not her own either. She usually laughed them off—except my father's; his were always serious.

Next morning, the whole finger was red and swollen. It hurt, and the pain got worse as the day went by. I didn't feel like playing and lay on my mattress waiting for my mother and Jerry to come home. They brought the evening meal but I had no appetite. In the middle of that night the pain woke me up. I got a cup of water in the dark and dunked the finger in to cool it. My mother turned on the light. The finger was now twice as thick as the others. The cut had turned yellow and was crusted shut; my body felt warm. She made a pan of hot water—the gas still worked in the kitchen—and put salt in it. She set the pan on the suitcase table. Jerry, now awake too, came and sat beside me and put his arm around my shoulder. My mother slowly placed my hand in the pan and told me to let it lie there. She said the hot salt water would soak the yellow dirt out of the cut. It was the dirt that was causing the swelling and the pain.

"It's not a little cut any more," she said. "It's a wound."

She sat at the end of her mattress by the dark lamp and the three of us talked in whispers so we wouldn't wake the others in the house. We each had a spoonful of sugar from our tin can with a lid. The water in the pan cooled and she heated more. The skin of my hand got soft and shrively but the wound stayed closed.

Early next morning before she went to work, my mother bandaged the finger and took me to see two nurses who lived in a garage. The nurses had grey hair, thick strong arms, and laughed a lot. One unwound my finger, held it up to the light, felt under my armpit, looked at the other nurse—and they both laughed, maybe to make me feel better. They gave me a piece of cold pancake but said that what I needed was lots of food and vitamins. This was their last pancake, though, and they certainly didn't have vitamins. My mother had to report to work so I trudged home and lay down on her mattress. I listened to insects in the hot air, watched *tjik-tjaks* zip after them on the walls. Lying so very still I had to think of my father's music "lessons." Sure, he had his "discipline," was always so certain he was right, and usually needed all attention for himself, but once, when I had sunstroke, he sat by my bed for hours holding my hand and somehow made himself so small that I wasn't aware of him as a person at all, only of my hand in his; he had been my daddy then. I missed him.

I didn't move on the mattress, but I was soaked in sweat. It was as if a clock was ticking inside my finger. My whole hand was fat and yellow and even my wrist was swollen and red. If I moved my arm even a little, it hurt. When my mother and Jerry came home they leaned over me and saw a thin line running from the finger across my hand and up my arm to the elbow. My mother wiped my forehead with a wet cloth and said, "That's blood poisoning."

She pressed her lips together. "We have to do something. Watch him," she said to Jerry, and went out. Jerry sat and looked at me, frowning, eyes warm, then began to read out loud from a book without pictures that I didn't understand.

My mother's lips were still thin when she returned. It was growing dark. She said she had talked to the nurses again. Drawing on me with her finger, she explained that the red line might run higher and higher up my arm, and then across my chest right to my heart. That was dangerous. Before that happened, the nurses had said, they would have to put me on a table and cut off my hand or even my arm.

"Well," said my mother, and she took my chin in her hand, "we don't want that. So you're going on a trip—tomorrow."

The houses and trees were still wrapped in mist when she and I walked hand in hand, which I wasn't used to any more, to a house near the camp gate; my wounded hand hung in a sling. A cock crowed, a free, early-morning plantation sound that we'd hear outside the walls of all our camps. My mother knocked on the door and a blonde girl in a thin grey dress that showed her panties opened it; inside the hallway a very old woman sat in a wheelchair with a blue woollen blanket spread over her knees.

"You're going to sit there on that little step," said my mother. "We're going to pull the blanket over you. Then we're going to wheel you down the street and through the gate. Somebody will lift this lady and you into a truck. The truck is going to a hospital where there's food and vitamins." The girl and the old woman were looking at me but didn't say anything.

"Stay under the blanket and be very quiet," my mother said. "If the soldiers at the gate catch you they might not let you or the lady out. Do you understand?" Then she took my face between her hands and kissed me long on one cheek and then on the other. "Remember," she said in my ear, "it's an adventure."

I climbed between the old woman's legs, the blanket came down, and the wheelchair began to move. It bumped out of the door and the bumps shot into my arm. It was hot under the blanket and the old woman smelled sour. We rolled along and no one said a word. We stopped and men's voices started shouting. There was a clank and a squeaking and the chair rolled on again and then it stopped. I felt us swing through the air and thump down, almost falling over—in the back of the truck, I guessed.

We started off. It was an old truck, like the one that brought us down from the mountains; its shaking shoved the chair around and at corners the old lady pressed her hands down on my head below her lap. In the blackness I squeezed my eyes shut against the pain from the jolting and from the heat of her legs. I sucked in my breath and held it longer, I'm sure, than ever in the swimming pool. It had to be so quiet at the pool now, all of us gone. I let myself float in the water, head down, arms dangling, cool, scanning the pale-green bottom: sometimes adults tossed coins in to dive after. When I came up for air I didn't move a muscle—there might be a soldier in the truck. I drifted away again.

We stopped. Outside I could hear only women's voices. "Careful, careful," said the old lady above. The blanket was lifted and my nose was in a long, wide, fresh-smelling white dress. I looked up. It was a tall woman wearing a huge stiff white cap that hid her hair. She bent forward and deep inside the cap, like in a little tunnel, I could see she was smiling and had red cheeks. "You look tired, little man," she said. Holding my good arm she helped me off the truck; a black cross on a silver chain swung from her neck. Other women in white dresses struggled with the wheelchair with the old lady in it. I never saw her again. The woman took my hand and as we walked down a long dark hall her dress whispered. At the end was a large room with many windows, full of beds in rows with children in them, and in the centre a small glass room. The woman pointed to an empty bed and said she would be right back. A bed with legs and sheets. I felt so heavy I could hardly climb onto it. The woman returned and gave me a cup of one of my favourite foods—fruit salad. I should call her "Sister," she said. She studied my yellow hand, not touching it, and said it would heal quickly with lots of food and vitamins. Now I should rest.

At midday a sister brought a tray with soup, rice, meat, gravy, corn, pudding, and more fruit salad and I ate on the bed like at home. With milk I swallowed pills from a tiny paper cup. I asked if I could keep the cup. She said yes, but now it was afternoon-sleep time; I wasn't used to being told what to do during the day.

Most of the children were still sleeping when the first sister came and took me into the glass room. It held a chair and a desk with a bowl of hot water on it. She started to explain, but I said there was salt in the bowl to soak out the dirt. Slowly, without help, I put my hand in it—and wanted to scream. She said I was brave; she would come back when the water was cold. And she whispered away. It hurt so much, I couldn't help it, I had to cry. I sat in the glass room several times a day for many days. Everybody, of course, could see me, so what I did then was sing as loud as I could with my hand in the water so no one would think I was crying. Over and over, I sang:

My bonnie lies over the ocean,
My bonnie lies over the sea,
My bonnie lies over the ocean,
Oh bring back my bonnie to me.

There are many words to this song, but I sang what I knew.

After that first soaking, I was told I was free to roam around, and found I was the healthiest and oldest child on the floor and the only one allowed out of bed. Many kids had tubes sticking out, some twitched, some whimpered, some lay still, staring. I touched a few and their skin burned.

In a little room by himself I discovered a boy about my age named Peter. He had a white face, hair so blond it was almost white, and huge blue eyes. His voice was high and loud. The bed sheet covered him up to his chin; he didn't move except sometimes to lift out his hands and rest them on his chest, thin hands. He told me at once that his left leg had been caught under the wheel of a moving van, the kind my mother pushed around; it happened before the camp, and buffalo had been pulling it. Under the sheet his leg lay inside a wire cage, specially built for it, that he never let me see. He smelled terrible, as bad as the boar's head when I buried it the second time. You couldn't escape his stink; I guessed he didn't notice it any more. I visited him often, stepping in and out of his room. He liked to talk and when I moved outside he just raised that sharp voice.

Peter was a favourite of the sisters. Every day they ran in to see him and say hello. They were very busy—in the night there would be the same face that I'd seen in the morning reading by a small lamp in the glass room—but there was always time for Peter. When sisters rushed by, I'd ask, "How's Peter?" and I'd get a smile.

You would think Peter liked the attention, but he didn't. He had heard the sisters discuss his leg when they thought he was asleep. He had already had three operations, but was sure his leg would be better soon; or they'd cut it off. One day, he told me, he would be a soldier—like his father who had been killed by the Japanese—and he knew positively you could be a soldier just as well on one leg. He would then talk about weapons, tanks, marching. He knew a lot but he never laughed; didn't smile even for the sisters. With no father and maybe having to live with one leg, he had to be sad inside, and scared. After months in hospital and three operations, the smashed leg still wasn't fixed; maybe it couldn't be; maybe his whole body hidden under that sheet was swollen and yellow and he would die. If my hand smelled bad up close and hurt like crazy, Peter's pain had to be a hundred times worse—too much for a kid. I didn't understand it. Did the sisters understand it? If I had had my harmonica with me, I would have given it to him.

What I didn't like was that Peter did all the talking, and was always so certain about everything. When I showed him my

hand on the first day he hardly looked at it. I should see his leg!
All I needed was food and vitamins. He overwhelmed me, yet he
was really only interested in himself.

That first night, alone after supper, sitting on my bed
watching the sun go down through the windows, homesickness
hit me. My mother, Jerry, our cozy dark room—it was like a
cramp in my stomach. I felt like running away. I could, too. I'd
done it before, when I was about six, right there in Bandung,
before the war, when my parents were out in the country for a
little holiday and Aunt Ina was looking after us; maybe Aunt Ina
had been strict with me that day. Jerry and I slept in the same
room, and the night before in the dark I had asked him the route
out of the city to the house of our parents' friends. He told me,
thinking I'd forget about it next day. But I didn't. I sneaked out
at dawn and walked and walked along dusty streets crowded with
horse-drawn carriages, cars, bicycles, and food stalls on the sidewalks, until I was lost. A policeman was sitting on his motorcycle
by the side of the road, so I asked him the way. Did my parents
know I was coming? No, it was a surprise. Well, it was far, and he
didn't think it a good idea. First he drove me sitting in his
sidecar to the police station, phoned Aunt Ina, then we rode
home. Hanneke, Ineke, Jerry, Aunt Ina holding Erik, and neighbours were outside waiting. I waved from the sidecar. But, inside,
Aunt Ina gave me an angry scolding, and Jerry, too.

I wasn't even homesick then, just missed my parents. I had
been really homesick the year before, when I was five—the very
first time I was away from home by myself. A couple of hours'
drive from our plantation, lived a rich family, also on a plantation, who kept riding horses. Because I'd been good, my parents
called and asked if I could come and stay for the weekend; I'd
never met them before. There was a father, a mother, and two

teenage daughters. I arrived in the morning and the man shook my hand, the woman and the two girls smiled; none of them said much. I was shown my room, the house, the stables. Then came lunch. A room with walls of dark wood, a long table set with shining glasses, napkins in silver holders, and in front of each plate a tiny pewter vase with flowers. The man sat at the head, the mother and I on one side, the daughters across from us. They bowed heads, folded hands, and prayed; I put my head down, too. Indonesians served food and left, and we began to eat. No one spoke. The man leaned his chin on one hand and ate with the other and stared ahead. When his mouth was closed, chewing slowly, it formed a half moon with the points down. He'd take another bite and the mouth would go down again. The woman and girls just smiled, passing things to each other, to him, to me. We were up to dessert and no one had said a word. It was at meals that we talked most at home. Were they waiting for me? Was I being impolite? "This is delicious," I said. The mother smiled and nodded. The girls smiled. The father stared, chewing. I kept quiet.

In the afternoon an Indonesian stable-hand walked me around the grounds on a saddled horse; he knew a lot about the animals, showed where they liked being stroked, told me to always talk softly near them. Dinner around the pretty table was as silent as lunch. At the end of the meal I looked out the window, saw the sun go down, and that strange, sad cramp rose up. Oh to be home! The father at that moment pushed his chair back and crooked his finger at me to follow him. He strode ahead to a room full of leather chairs and a couch; the top of a heavy desk was also leather and books lined the walls even over a fireplace. On the desk was a phone and he dialled a number and handed the phone to me. My mother answered. The man was standing a few feet away. I told her what a great wonderful time I was having, I had ridden a brown horse, brushed it after. The man walked to the end of the room and lifted a book from a shelf. "Mommie," I whispered, "come get me quick!" Well, she would, of course, she said, but it was almost night now and I knew how narrow the roads were. She missed me, too, and so did Daddy and Jerry. Tomorrow, if I wanted to, I could call again. Okay? Sleep well, *jochie*.

The next day the stable-hand helped me ride the same horse and sometimes even let go of it. I sat through the prayers and silent meals, smiled, and thought my own thoughts. After supper the father crooked his finger again. He lit a fire in his room and we sat on the leather couch leafing through books with pictures of horses. In the morning, settled in the front of their car with the chauffeur, I waved goodbye to the family, the mother and daughters smiling, the father not.

It had grown dark in the hospital. A sister sat reading in the glass room. I went to sleep.

It took seventeen days for my wound to heal. In the late afternoon of the last day the sisters hoisted me up into the back of a truck full of mothers and children going to the camp for the first time. When we got to the gate it had grown almost dark. The soldiers yelling at the women and children to get off the truck didn't notice the extra boy. My mother and Jerry had come to the gate every evening, which was when new prisoners arrived, and they were waiting. My mother kissed me long on both cheeks and laughed and said, "Thank God for small mercies," and Jerry smiled his crooked smile. I showed them my finger right away. It was the same as the other fingers, except the skin over the knuckle wasn't rimpled but smooth and showed a tiny pink line no bigger than an eyelash.

FOUR / Christmas 1942

IN A HOT COUNTRY people rise early because the first hours are coolest. Mist shreds, cocks cry, and in the camp's crowded houses women and children shuffle out of stuffy rooms to line up for toilets.

If I just had to pee, I went behind two old banana trees in the back yard; nobody noticed. I could have used the toilet that morning without waiting because it was dark out. Nothing stirred. Stars still blinked. I had woken up and couldn't lie on my mattress a second longer. That day we were going to have, as my mother said, "a hell" of a party—the first one in camp. I couldn't believe I was the only one up, but peed in the yard anyway.

For days special food had been sneaked into the house; I'd smelled some of it already being cooked on the gas stove. And I'd heard women and older girls squealing behind closed doors. What was going on there? The evening before, floors had been mopped, windows washed, ledges dusted, and cans, bottles, glasses, even a bucket filled with flowers and weeds and set out where the party would be—in the front hall and in Mrs Witte's room. Scrounged chairs lined the hallway; a scarred Chinese lantern dangled from the ceiling. But giving it all away was what my friend Mrs Plomp had brought in: a Christmas tree made of thick paper. It stood in a place of honour next to the piano. The tree had "snow" painted on its green needles, hanging ribbons, a silver star on top, and small red real candles. They would be lit, she'd promised.

I sat down in the dark in front of our door and exercised my calf muscles. I did this in quiet moments: in bed, on the toilet, listening to my mother or Jerry read. I kept at it; I kneaded the muscles, tensed them and let go, tensed and let go. Strength mattered; calves had become important. I looked out for them; I still walked head down, as in the days when scanning for metal, so I saw feet and calves first. I knew, I suppose, that people's eyes and mouths and voices were more telling, but I liked calves. Thick and round, jumping with power, muscles straining. Some Japanese guards and big boys and surprisingly many women and older girls had them, but few children. From before the war I remembered the sweating *betja* men pedalling their carrier tricycles around Bandung—those were calves! I needed a set. I would work and work on my calf muscles and they would swell up. It was a matter of time. It was also something I couldn't talk about. It wasn't a secret like building the steamship, but it still had to be kept quiet.

It wasn't just that I wanted first-class calves for myself; I enjoyed good calves, enjoyed looking at them, whoever they belonged to. In a few months I would come to live next door to the finest calves in the world. I would watch them in marvellous action; many would—and maybe see more than just calves. But I got to know the calves' owner and I always felt that, privately, she was proud of them. And she had a right to be. Time, though, would go by in the camps, and calves would lose out to breasts.

A day bird tested its voice against the fading night, and others took it up. From behind the camp's wall, a cock shouted he was on duty. Stumblings and mutterings followed from the house, from our room too—and it wasn't even light yet. They hadn't forgotten! Jerry clumped out straight for the toilet, probably thinking he was up first. The day of the party had begun.

Had the camp been given the day off? Was it a Sunday? Anyhow, everybody was home, and busy: cooking, tidying, even raking the gravel path to the front door, scurrying in and out of each other's rooms. Again that hush-hush giggling. It wasn't surprise gifts; I knew that the Dutch didn't give presents on Christmas. Gifts came from St Nicholas on December 5, the old Spanish saint's birthday. I'd been told that every year he sailed from Spain into Amsterdam harbour in the bow of a ship, astride a white horse, dressed in scarlet cape and mitre, clutching a curved staff, white beard blowing, smiling and waving at hordes of singing but nervous children on the docks. Black manservants surrounded him, shaking white-gloved fingers and birch bundles at the kids in a threatening way. If you'd been good, you got treats, presents, and teasing, funny little gifts. If you'd been bad, well, tough luck.

Christmas was more serious. It was the day God's son, Jesus, was born. He died with nails hammered through his hands and feet on a cross; for us, I had been told. He was a good man who loved children and said everybody should; also your neighbours and your enemies. My mother made me promise to bathe thoroughly, soap the armpits, soap the crotch, put on clean shorts, wear a shirt—and sandals. What! How would I ever get feet like Manang's then? She said it was just for one day, you dressed up for parties, and, besides, Jesus wore sandals. No arguments: she had a lot on her mind.

And she did. Besides cooking and cleaning, readying Jerry, me, and herself, she had taken on a bunch of us kids to perform "Hark the Herald Angels Sing" that afternoon. We couldn't party after dark for fear of alerting the Japanese; visitors also had to slip in just one or two at a time. As it was, the smells of frying onions, chicken, bacon, and bananas, baking cookies, and roasting peanuts wafted out. The women had all dug out money or swapped stuff for the food treats. If soldiers came they'd throw the food out or cart it away. Were parties like ours going on all over the camp? You couldn't tell.

For about a week, when she had time after work, my mother had gathered Ineke, Hanneke, Jerry, me, and four other kids in the back yard and taught us the English hymn, singing softly so it would be a surprise for the others. None of us understood English, except Jerry who knew a little, but my mother had been a teacher in Canada and was a good explainer if not a great singer. We understood the words now and could sing them to her tune very well. Still, she wanted one more rehearsal, so we went through it again in the garden. Her hair was braided around her head and she wore a dress in her favourite colour, green, a thin white belt, white earrings, white sandals, and lipstick. She didn't own lipstick and I was pretty sure the earrings were Mrs Witte's.

The women and girls had all borrowed and switched clothes and jewellery—that was the to-do behind doors. And I had to admit they looked fresh and nice and smelled of soap; Ineke and Hanneke, too, in ironed blouses and skirts, hair damp from bathing. I didn't often look at Ineke and Hanneke closely because, well, they were sisters. We were in all the same camps, but I didn't play with them much because they were older, and working, and girls—and I never noticed them growing into young women. In the Bloemenkamp days, though, when things weren't so bad yet, they always did look neat: Aunt Ina was set on that. She liked order and tidiness and would fret about it. She was often ill and then my mother might go over and do the wash. I was there once when Aunt Ina asked if she would please also iron the sheets and pillow cases, and my mother said, "Certainly not."

Eating started. The hallway and Mrs Witte's room were packed full and half dark with the shutters closed against the sun; but the crowd gave off its own heat and soon the few sweet whiffs of perfume were gone. We ate standing up; there weren't enough plates, so children ate from banana leaves. We ate and ate, and it was quiet. Besides a big bowl of peanuts, there was a lot of avocado salad, fried rice, and fruit salad; adults weren't watching, and I overdid it. But I wasn't the only one.

Dishes were piled up in the kitchen, and we hurried back into the hallway and Mrs Witte's room. Wearing a pale yellow dress and high heels, Mrs Plomp had matches ready and we oohed and aahed as each candle came to life. The tree's flickering brightness bathed the women and children pressed together. Mrs Plomp's smiling, sweating face shone in the light and she looked oh, lovely. Maybe, just then, we all did.

At that moment the damn tree said, "Whooosh!" and was gone in one great lick of flame. There were screams and people jostled to trample on burning bits and candle stubs. But nothing, not the wall, not the piano or the blankets around it to muffle the sound, was even singed, just a small spot on the floor, a little. And then there was laughter. We started to clap our hands and cheer and someone whistled on her fingers. It was a party!

A chair was placed where the tree had been and Mrs Witte sat down with a book. Everybody made themselves comfortable. Mrs Witte wearing a white dress crossed her longer leg over the other, opened the book, and in her soft, polite way began to read the story of the birth of Jesus. It was a children's book and when she came to a picture she would pause to hold it up for us to see, then go on reading. Sitting on the floor Jerry and I leaned against the legs of our mother seated on a chair behind us. I had heard the story before and Mrs Witte was not a good reader; perhaps too polite to speak up. I flexed my calf muscles, let go, flexed, let go. Jesus, when he was older, said we should love everybody. Okay. What about Dirk? And the kite hunters? Well, Dirk, maybe. But what about the Japanese? Love Johnny Tomato, the guards, the commandant? They were the enemy! My mother had said so, again and again. But Jesus had especially mentioned enemies. Had He ever been in a camp though? Had He seen the Japanese beating women and girls? They could be Ineke, Hanneke, Aunt Ina, Mrs Plomp, Mrs Witte—my mother. Men shouldn't hit women. How many times hadn't Jerry and I been told that when Ineke or Hanneke pestered us? Did Jesus maybe have fear spirits in him like Manang's? To hate you needed to be brave, I thought, and I was sure I hated the Japanese: they were the enemy. I'd been told Jesus even loved the men who nailed Him to the cross.

Mrs Witte shut the book then, smiled, and said, "Now we're going to sing." She was a little the boss at the party.

A woman sat down at the piano and we all moved and stood around her. She set several music books on the ledge in front of her, opened one, and began to play. The piano sounded dull. We sang along with her, all Dutch Christmas songs, but kept our voices down. They were familiar songs and we'd sung about six, when Mrs Witte said, "Anna?"

My mother and the eight of us grouped together.

The woman at the piano asked what we were going to sing.

"Hark the Herald Angels Sing."

"Oh, I have that!" said the woman, and she switched her music book for another and flipped the pages.

"Damn!" murmured my mother.

"Sing along with me—*me!*" she whispered to us. "Don't listen to the piano!"

"Ah," said the woman. She spread the book out on the ledge and began to play.

We joined her and for a few lines we were fine, but the piano seemed to go faster or higher, and we stumbled. We tried to catch up, but couldn't, and then, one by one, we children stopped—and my mother was singing alone. We looked at her; everyone did. She wasn't in tune with the music but she kept on singing. The piano stopped, and the woman turned around. In her not perfect voice my mother sang her English song—the only non-Dutch person there. She sang on, unseeing, tears streaming down her face. I'd never seen her cry before and wouldn't again in the camps. When she finished, it was very still, and she ran out of the hallway.

FIVE / Empire of the Sun

THE SUN WAS THE FRIEND of the Japanese. Even their flag was white with a red sun in the middle. Jerry hated it, didn't want to see it. But it was the only flag and fluttered from poles on the soccer field, in front of the commandant's house, the guards' stations, the administration building, the camp gate; it was in our eyes daily. The Japanese used the sun to hurt us. Day in day out they let it burn down for long hours on workers, weakening and dulling them. A prisoner who broke a rule might be dragged to a shadeless spot to stand at attention, or sit there hunched up in a little bamboo cage, for a day, or two days, eyes burning, lips cracking, with no food or water and kicks and slaps if she blacked out.

Called to the soccer field once again to listen to the commandant, we waited half the afternoon in the sun, people moaning, leaning on each other, no sitting, then jerking straight to bow as, suddenly, he was striding past with his men, sword swinging, boots shining, and making his jump onto the platform. Via the young woman interpreter, he yelled first, as usual, that we were the enemies of Nippon, that only through the goodness of the Emperor were we housed and fed, that we had no home and fatherland any more—"and so you have no religion any more"—and that we must be obedient, polite, humble, and self-disciplined; on and on.

I had begun to find it hard to pay attention at these meetings; afterwards I had to ask what had been said. I watched, instead—the commandant, the officers, the soldiers, the translator, the dusty field of women and children from which the heat trembled upward blurring their faces, the flag above, ants scrambling across my feet. It wasn't just difficult to listen, something in me didn't want to. It wasn't especially because it was a Japanese forcing me—although maybe that's how it started; my mind also wandered when, say, one of the women administrators, just another prisoner, called us together; even when a bunch from our house was chatting on the front steps in the evening, and I kept my eyes glued on the speaker, I would lose track. If I was brought in then with a question, I'd feel dopey; it would get worse, this weird resistance to the grip of another's voice. It didn't happen with those who were close; and I was fine with one or two or three people: a good listener.

Did the commandant have a mother? Was she a yeller? Did he yell back? Did he beat his own wife and children? Or not. Did he miss them terribly? Or not. Was the interpreter his girlfriend? People said so. She watched the commandant bellowing and when he paused and turned to her she'd still be looking up at him, and I saw before she spoke her lips sometimes move a tiny bit, almost in a smile, as if she agreed, as if she thought he was clever; but maybe she was just nervous. She had to be careful, she was a prisoner, too, and thousands of eyes were on her—the commandant was the enemy. "Don't smile at the enemy," my mother had said. Jesus, of course, said, "Love them." What was a "girlfriend"? Probably many of those thousands of eyes, like Jerry's, didn't want to look at the Japanese flag either. None of them, certainly, wanted to look into Japanese eyes. The officers and soldiers stood on either side of the platform, faces closed, but you felt them watching. Once, an officer had suddenly turned to the soldiers behind him pointing to someone standing in the front row. Two soldiers trotted up to a middle-aged woman, grabbed her, and ran her, stumbling and sagging between them, off the field. The other Japanese didn't move. A few days later on the street I spotted the woman rewinding a piece of bed sheet into a turban around her shaven head, her face still blotched and swollen. She had looked into the officer's eyes, I bet. Were the ants at my feet as uninterested in us as the stars at night? A girlfriend might be a girl you could look at naked.

The translator said we must all be at the gate with our belongings early next morning. Then the commandant leapt down and we bowed.

I looked at my mother.

"Moving to Tjihapit!" she whispered. Tjihapit was another section of Bandung also fenced off into a camp, but bigger. The interpreter warned us to bring only what we could carry, not counting mattresses, and not to smuggle anything forbidden— Dutch paper money or coins, any orange ornament (for Holland's House of Orange), pictures of the royal family, cutting tools, foreign flags, radio parts, books, paper, pens and pencils, and so on. There would be searches. And to wear our numbers! At some time in Bloemenkamp we were given numbers. My mother stitched ours on rectangular bits of cloth and sewed them on our pants; mine was 12952.

Why were we moving? Rumours raced. The Japanese were winning, they were losing. Tjihapit was awful, a punishment camp; no, it was better, only three families per house. Nobody knew. There was no explanation.

Well, I didn't care. At least there was action! For me the worst thing about living in Bloemenkamp was not the heat, fear, smells, noise, flies, too many bodies, too little food, scratches that festered, and diarrhea—it was the sameness. The days and weeks and months had dragged by. Women and older children at least swept streets, cooked, cleaned sewers, moved furniture. Mostly on my own, I had sleeps in the middle of the day, wandered around camp, usually unafraid now with my laugh, and sat in shadowy places staring. It was even a relief, it seemed sometimes, that there were always new no-nos: no lights on after eight, no wood-gathering for cooking fires, no meeting in groups, absolutely no *gedekken* through the wall; on and on. But just as the Japanese would get tougher right until the end, some people would disobey right until the end and, for example, smuggle anyway—a few because they were brave and generous, others because they were greedy. And they got us all into trouble.

Packing for us was simple: we had less than what we had carried down from the plantation; it all fitted easily into our three rucksacks and suitcases. The only "thing" I owned was the little harmonica in its handkerchief. But there were people living near Bandung who had entered camp with servants pushing piled-high handcarts. One woman, who was a professor, had come with seven cabin trunks full of books. And there were those, like Dirk and his mother, whose home had already been in Bloemenkamp. They had one night to decide what to take; but that's all we'd had, too, wasn't it? Dirk would have to leave behind most of his toys, of course—certainly his lead soldiers. Too heavy. Now he would know what it was like to have no toys, and no soldiers. Maybe, though, his mother should let Dirk keep two or three so he could at least play by himself. They wouldn't take much space. He could carry them in his pocket. Maybe she would.

Early next morning we marked the mattresses with our numbers and piled them up in front of the house for a truck to pick up. Too late I remembered the rat I'd buried in the back yard; maybe someone else would enjoy its little, white skeleton. When we arrived at the gate there was already a long line-up, six or seven women and children across, many wearing several layers of clothing, surrounded by backpacks, suitcases, bags, baskets, sacks made of knotted-up bed sheets, and trunks. Trunks, of course, needed two carriers, but there was no rule about that. Dangling from women's bodies and from their luggage I saw pots, pans, kettles, water canteens, pails, tubs, purses, a chicken-feather duster, a carpet-beater, a hat, a clock, and a doll. Some had brought bird cages with birds in them, rolled-up rugs, fold-up chairs, musical instruments, even a tire from a car. Stuff! How were they going to lug it all? What I didn't know was that Tjihapit's gate was almost across the street from ours.

We nudged luggage forward, a foot maybe, and stopped. Far in front on wobbly bamboo tables outside the gate soldiers rooted through every piece of luggage, taking their time, fingering, shaking out. Once directed, the Japanese slogged away at a job with stiff purpose, rain or shine, entirely absorbed. The sun rose higher; luckily for those overdressed people, there was a breeze. I heard a small scream behind us, then crying: with a rag a mother was wiping off brown trickles running down the legs of her teenage daughter; nothing to cry about really. Murmurs reached us from up front that there was smuggling going on. Several times, way ahead, we heard bursts of yelling and we all tensed up: somebody caught.

When we got closer to the gate I saw two young women standing to the side, straggly hair falling over puffy, bloodied faces, their clothes streaked with red earth—so the soldiers had been mad enough to beat them to the ground. That anger would increase with the day's growing heat. No one, of course, dared approach the women or call to them, and they didn't look up. We said nothing to each other, just shuffled past, but the line-up moved so slowly everyone had a long look at them. I even turned to stare, until my mother twisted my head straight. The whole day the two would shake and sway there trying to stay on their feet; all of Bloemenkamp would file by them. We heard later they had collapsed a few times and been kicked upright again.

Only three rows away from the gate my mother suddenly started groping around in her mesh bag. "Damn it!" she muttered. Then she yanked out something in a pale green handkerchief, held by a knot on top. Looking ahead, as if her hands at her side didn't belong to her, she untied the cloth and slowly, slowly let it slip open.

Not slowly enough! First the woman beside her sneezed, then someone behind her. My mother sneezed, I sneezed, Jerry sneezed—and then everybody around us was sneezing. Taking deep breaths and pinching their noses, wiping their noses on hands and sleeves.

"I'm so sorry, so sorry!" whispered my mother, twirling around so all of us could hear. She wore a faded brown dress that looked too big on her. "It's pepper. I found a whole box. I was going to smuggle it—but I changed my mind. Pepper! Sorry!"

Ten, fifteen, maybe twenty women and children were standing around sneezing, sneezing like mad, eyes watering, coughing, and then one of them started to laugh, and the next second all of us sneezers were laughing. The story of the sneezers raced down the line-up—past the two punished women—and a wave of laughter came back, and then another.

The soldiers looked up from behind their loaded tables into the faces of hundreds of laughing prisoners. Their expressions unreadable, their black eyes flitted to and fro. Did they think the laughter was directed at them? Much less had sparked terrible rage. No. It was just a clutch of women and children sneezing up front. Still, it must have made them angry, but what could they do? Wade in and slap all those laughing mouths? They bent down again to fussing with clothes and hairbrushes and family snapshots.

SIX / Tjihapit

OUR NEW CAMP, Tjihapit, held about 15,000 prisoners, three times as many as Bloemenkamp. Bigger in size, it was also a lot more crowded. It swallowed neighbours and friends; many I never saw again: Mrs Witte and Mieke, Dirk, and Mrs Plomp. Since Aunt Ina, Erik, Ineke, and Hanneke were allotted a room some distance from us we seldom visited.

At first, in Tjihapit, time moved fast: everything and everybody was new. Eleven other families lived in our house and it had one toilet. Our room (which in her way our mother at once made a safe space) was about the same size as the one in Bloemenkamp—the mattresses just fit—but it had a window. We looked out on the back yard over a round flower bed, as high and wide as a truck tire, thick with orange and pink hibiscus, and on to a clump of short fruitless palm trees.

Jerry and I went to explore. Besides the palms growing in a tight circle, which formed a decent cave, the garden held two low, climbable trees, and more useless flower beds. Never mind if Johnny Tomato might also move to Tjihapit, the beds would have to be dug up and planted with vegetables. An overgrown lawn ringed the house and in the rear, on our side, it stretched a dozen steps to the edge of a stinking sewer; on the other side of the ditch rose the camp's bamboo fence. Open sewers ran behind all the houses but were usually hidden by man-high whitewashed walls topped with spikes or shards of glass to stop thieves. The foot-wide ditches, with a walkway on either side for cleaners (before the war), made a network of alleys throughout the camp. After a rainstorm, the sewers, not built to service the thousands now crammed into that small section of Bandung, quickly overflowed and the alleys turned into narrow foaming rivers. Some people threw garbage, broken glass, wrecked furniture and appliances, used-up bicycles, anything at all, over those walls. So, when the sun came out and the water level sank, there could be interesting finds amongst the steaming debris; flies, snakes, rats, snails, ravens, and frogs that honked in the night thought so, too. It was stupid to forage there on bare feet and we clappered walking in *klompen,* pieces of wood carved to fit soles and held on by strips of rubber tire across the toes. One girl didn't and stepped on a nail: awful poisons raced through her body and she was soon dead.

Ours was a corner house on a hilly street that climbed towards us and stopped short at the camp's wall. Beyond it was the "outside," from which in the quiet of the evening sometimes drifted sounds, faint and unreal: horseshoes on pavement, a *betja* bell, a vendor's cry nearing and fading. Camp streets were busy with women and teenagers walking to and from work or fetching food, children playing, women pushing the creaking moving vans, and, infrequently, soldiers on bicycles or in a car or truck. Already grass and weeds sprouted from Tjihapit's cracked sidewalks and pitted streets, cut telephone lines drooped from poles, and scum crusted the surface of clogged roadside ditches. Except for vegetable patches, gardens grew wild beneath wash lines strung up helter-skelter. Houses showed broken windows, doors and shutters askew, dangling eavestroughs, peeling paint, sunken roofs, and holes knocked into outside walls as additional entrances; inside, plaster crumbled, roofs leaked, and electrical wiring, plumbing, and gas piping had failed. It would get worse, but we wouldn't notice.

My mother was ordered to chop vegetables in the kitchen. Everybody, of course, wanted to work there—and often those who did looked fitter than the rest. But the preparing and ladling out of food was strictly supervised by certain women who had to report again to the women who ran the camp's administration. Thieves were fired and everyone heard of it. Once, maybe twice, my mother hid a carrot in her clothes and brought it home, but she said it wasn't worth it. She did still manage, though, to get hot water for her important afternoon tea. "It's hard to stay alive," she said, "but even harder to stay alive and decent." I stole anyway, unripe fruit mostly. By now I often stilled her voice in my mind.

Weeks flowed into months and the terrible sameness of Bloemenkamp took over in Tjihapit too. Heat enervated; only in sleep would food not nag at your mind; the air was thick with smells and flies; and here, too, roamed the gangs of Indo boys. Fear grew: the Japanese and the *heihos*—uniformed young Indonesians in their service—became angry more quickly and slapped and kicked and punished women for the slightest misconduct. *Gedekken,* smuggling, was now seen as a real crime, though it didn't stop. Once Ineke, at fourteen, actually had the nerve to sneak out of Tjihapit through a sewer alley and carry back fruit. If caught she, and probably Aunt Ina too, would have been beaten and shaved, at the very least. Sometimes a woman, without being allowed to pack or say goodbye to her children, was just hauled out of camp. That usually meant the *Kempetai*— and the end of her. The Germans had the Gestapo, the Japanese the *Kempetai*. They were the military police who beat with whips, tore out fingernails, burned with cigarettes, and killed. When a *Kempetai* officer wandered into camp, it got cold.

Jerry had at once been put to work too, of course. His job was pulling carts with other boys his age, collecting garbage. Quickly rotten in the heat and covered with flies, the piles of rubbish had to be picked up mostly by hand; there were no shovels. But there was a good side: sometimes you found stuff. Jerry would hide his prizes in a bush and retrieve them later.

Extremely important to scrounge at that time were wheels. Bicycle wheels and roller-skate wheels—roller skating had been popular before the war. Jerry was always on the lookout for them on his rounds; me too, on treks through the warren of sewer alleys. If you had wheels, enough of them, you could begin to build one of two types of vehicle that kids had somehow hit upon in Tjihapit: "velos" and "tanks."

There were only three or four velos in the entire camp and they belonged to the oldest boys. Even to be able to say you slightly knew a velo owner was an honour: he had respect. To make a velo you had to have filched all sorts of materials and tools, and you needed know-how. A velo was the size of a small car, made up of four bicycle wheels fixed to the front and back of a frame of two-by-fours. Two bicycle chains running on the back wheels and two sets of pedals (for driver and passenger sitting roughly in the middle) propelled it; and a car's steering wheel and shaft wired to the front wheels gave control. I never rode on a silently whizzing-along velo—it must have been so fine. Older girls liked velos. They smiled at the drivers.

Ankie Crone was an older girl, about fourteen, and I'd seen her smile at Polo who was the owner of a velo. Ankie was one of Mrs Crone's three children; the family lived in the room next to ours. Harry, at fifteen the oldest, tall and bony like his mother but unlike her not a talker, had already decided to become a seaman. His father, a ship's captain who, I noticed in photographs looked a head shorter than his wife, had been away at sea when the Japanese invaded and nobody knew where he was. Greddie, eleven, also tall, I didn't pay much attention to because, well, there wasn't much of my attention left after Ankie.

The Crones were remarkable in that, although thoroughly Dutch from the northern province of Groningen, they all had dark, slanted eyes. Ankie had a way of speaking and smiling at the same time, her pink cheeks narrowing her eyes to slits. When her face closed she looked thoughtful, older. But she smiled easily, mouth open, showing large white teeth; sometimes a small moan escaped her throat. It was a treat. In the first days, I watched her face, waiting. But as we all got to know each other—Mrs Crone and my mother would become best friends—I began to try to make her smile, at me. I learned that, while her smile might come quickly, for serious Ankie there always had to be a reason: the smile was a sort of reward. So, when I saw her smile at Polo, I knew it couldn't be just because of his dumb velo.

Older girls ignored tanks, as did most younger ones. Tanks were for boys, rough boys, or boys who were maybe a little crazy. For a tank you needed at least one and a half roller skates or three pairs of wheels (better if you had a full set though). From odd pieces of plank a sturdy floor was hammered together, about as big as a cabin trunk, under which at the rear end two pairs of wheels were fastened. The third pair was screwed at the mid-point of a separate board bolted with some play beneath the centre of the floor's front end; that board, with rope running from either end through holes in the floor, allowed steering. Then, to the height of a crouched boy, the front, sides, and roof were nailed up with anything heavy and strong—wood, metal, flat stones—and wound around and around with wire, even barbed wire; long nails, slammed in from inside, stuck out from the sides. Especially reinforced was the tank's front end. A gash was cut at eye level for the driver to see through. Entry was from the open back.

One day Jerry found a single set of little wheels on his garbage route; a week later we dug up a whole roller skate in a sewer alley. We could start but we needed patience because Jerry was gone for most of the day. I wandered eyes down along the streets and through the sewer alleys scanning for discarded wood and metal as in the old days I had collected for the ship of my dreams. I ripped off the doors of a toaster, straightened bent nails with a rock. Because our street was a dead-end, the last few hundred yards, the stretch below our house up to the top of a small hill, had very little traffic. Jerry and I studied that dip in the road. It had possibilities.

About two months went by, and slowly beneath our window, the machine grew. Mostly it was Jerry's work and his planning. Just as when he built the kite, I sat watching him as I used to watch Manang. Like our father, he had clever, sure hands; like Manang he said little. One afternoon he returned with the side of a small icebox: just what we needed. I unearthed a hunk of car tire: perfect. A thin, red-haired boy from our house named Willie, about my age, lent a pair of pliers for twisting wire. A tank was taking shape. It was getting dark, and when he straightened up, Jerry grinned and gave it a couple of good kicks. "Almost," he said, pleased with himself.

My mother watched us through the window. I'm not sure she even knew what we were up to. As on the plantation when we were busy hunting panthers or burying Leo she let us be.

She had asked what I wanted for my eighth birthday coming up in a day or so. What a question. What was there to give? I said I would like a fruit salad.

But when I woke up that day, there was a traditional Dutch birthday chair, a chair she'd borrowed (we didn't have one) all decorated with flowers and bits of coloured paper stuck on with the glue-like porridge we were fed. The two of them sang Happy Birthday. On the chair's seat, each with a bit of white ribbon around it, were a pencil and a child's drawing pad. My mother handed me a cup of fruit salad. "There's more tonight," she promised. Who knows how she got the fruit, the presents, and the ribbon.

"Hey—look," said Jerry and pointed out the window. Our monster vehicle had been wheeled to the middle of the lawn; palm leaves lay across the top with a scrap of cardboard tucked upright between them that said: ERNEST'S TANK. That was Jerry for you.

My brother told me he had set up a "race" after work that same day. We'd really have to practise hard when he got home because the other guys were coming around six. That afternoon I climbed inside the tank and Jerry gave it a hard, long push. The weight of the thing made it rumble down our hill terrifically fast, but it listened sharply to my jerking on the ropes— the power of it! Then together we pulled it back up and I went down again and again; Jerry took one ride himself.

The day was cooling and some women and children came out to watch; our mother did, Mrs Crone did, Ankie did—would she think I was pretty brave? And right at six, there appeared a tank and some boys at the top of the opposite hill. Shouting, Jerry made it clear that he would give the starting signal with a towel. He called to a few neighbour boys to help him push.

"Get in, kid," he said.

I wriggled inside and knelt, dripping sweat, forehead pressed against the piece of car tire, eyes locked on the lookout slit. I felt a jolt and at once the tank was rolling fast, then faster and faster, little wheels roaring, and I heard myself screaming— the wild feel of it rocketing down! And plunging from the other hill, just as fast, the enemy. My tank obeyed my every tug to the last second—and so did his. And when we plowed head-on into each other there was a great crunching, cracking, and clattering. The tanks fell apart around us drivers and running down the hills came our crews, jumping, yelping, and thumping each other.

We'd done it. Never mind the stupid flies, the stink, being hungry or sick all the time, or the *Kempetai*. We'd done it. Maybe we were just numbers who had only to bow. But we had worked a long time to build a fine tank and then in a split second marvellously smashed that tank to pieces—because we damn well felt like it.

SEVEN / Willie

IN THAT PLACE where so much was breaking down and wearing out there was a boy who made things whole again.

Willie, his mother, and his older sister who played the accordion were already living in the big house when we came. Outside the door of their windowless room ran an open gully that carried everybody's bath and wash water to the sewage ditch. It was an airless storage room, or *gudang,* like the one we had had in Bloemenkamp. Why they hadn't grabbed our room when it was free, I'll never know. I once overheard a woman in our house, Mrs Slierendrecht, refer to Willie's mother's "humble origin." I didn't understand what she meant, so for a while I thought it was "humbleness" that had stopped Willie's mother from moving into a better room. The sisters in the hospital had talked about being humble; God liked it, they said.

I should have known better, of course, than to think Mrs Slierendrecht would ever say anything about anybody that wasn't meant to be nasty. Her thoughts were ashes. A tall, meaty, red-faced woman, she stomped to and from the toilet, chest out as if she were a queen, in a loose silk housecoat showing hunks of thigh and breast, yellow-grey hair flopping in an untidy braid. No one liked the toilet line-up: because so many had diarrhea there were accidents, but after a while you hardly noticed any more. Mrs Slierendrecht hated the line-ups and always said so. She complained, argued, and mentioned unkind things about people until the door shut behind her. And then she sat there a long time, it seemed to me. When she came out she marched by without a word. From the beginning she and her two grown-up, silent daughters had lived in the best room, in front, with windows. I thought Mrs Slierendrecht was crazy, but wasn't sure. She had a high Dutch accent and didn't have to go out to work, perhaps because she was over fifty, but she let on it was because she was a lady. Often I heard yelling behind their door.

Maybe Willie's mother had kept their room because it was separate from the rest of us, private. She was polite but didn't mix; waited to go until there was no line-up. How "humble origin" fitted her, I had no idea. She was a worried-looking woman, though. When she was home she didn't bother Willie—nobody did that—but she kept a sharp eye on him.

Straddling the gully in front of Willie's door were a small kitchen table and a chair protected from sun and rain by a black umbrella with its handle nailed to the table. Soapy water flowing beneath him, this is where Willie spent his days, shoulders rounded, very still, milk-blue eyes fixed on his small fussing fingers. He was shorter than me, skinny, freckled, flop-eared, with thin red hair that grew in tufts; it looked as if he was losing it. His mother made him wear a straw hat, but as soon as she was gone, he'd take it off—no, tear it off. It made him angry.

His mother and sister had jobs, so, like me, he was a lot on his own. I played, visited, fought, stole fruit, roamed the streets, and scavenged in alleys, but Willie had real work. Adults asked for his help and paid him, if they could, with food. Not yet nine, Willie had respect. And this is why: he could repair watches and clocks. He had the little tools, a magnifying glass he could screw in his eye, and a drawer in the table crammed with clock insides, broken watches, and tiny screws and springs and other parts.

Willie's customers came by in late afternoon from all over Tjihapit. He was praised, touched—from which he would bend away—and thanked. He spoke little and curtly, and only about the person's watch or clock; he seldom raised his eyes. Sometimes a piece was beyond repair and Willie would say so with certainty and no concern. Later, he might bring an oil lamp out to the table and keep at it after dark.

This is what Willie did and all he did. When I, at first, sitting by him began stories about the plantation or Bloemenkamp or people I knew, his silence stopped me; he didn't care. If I asked him a question, he'd move his head yes or no or answer in just a few words. I learned little. No, his father wasn't a planter; he worked for the railroad. No, his sister never played her accordion now. Yes, he had always lived in Bandung. And this was his reply to what everybody wanted to know: "I sort of picked it up."

I used to just sit in his doorway for a while and watch him tinkering, eyes inches from the table; he would swing his head in my direction to show he knew I was there. Then I'd wander off: Willie didn't need company. But I'd come back.

One day I went and stood behind him and leaned over. He was snipping off a piece of a very small spiral spring.

"Why?" I asked. That's all. Why?

"Because otherwise it won't fit in here, see?" said Willie promptly and pointed to a little open tunnel in a watch, one of a dozen lying around the table.

"But it's still too big!"

Willie turned and looked up at me.

"No," he said, "look." He picked up the cut spring with tweezers that pressed it down, then tucked the spring in the channel of the watch where it jumped taut.

"There," said Willie. "And now?"

"We're done," he said, and pressed the back plate of the watch into place with a click, shook it, and put it to his ear. He reached up and held it to my ear. I heard the watch ticking. It was as if Willie had stroked my cheek.

I found a pail and set it upside down beside him. In the next hour or so, as Willie puttered on, everything he did he explained, with words and by showing with his small tools; a really dumb question also got a sort of cackle. Each problem, once he'd solved it, was so simple; but the next one looked horribly complicated. Willie seemed years and years older than I.

I began to spend a lot of time on the pail, peering into watches and clocks, as Willie tightened, filed, cleaned, and murmured whys and hows and wheres. I had a share in the patience he had for his watches. Heads together we'd travel right into a timepiece, Willie leading but not far ahead, stopping to let me catch up, this way, that, and around. And then suddenly it was ticking again—alive. He allowed me to handle his tools; he let me, once, twice, and then more often, do a chore alone. I did well. An alarm clock bell rang again because of me. The hands on a pocket watch now could be relied on. "First class," said Willie. I progressed. This is how far: I once actually set in motion the stuck wheel-works of a watch set in a ring.

But Willie worried me. A few times, in the middle of work, he had suddenly, angrily, got up and saying nothing walked into his room and shut the door. I knocked, he didn't answer, so I left. Later he would only say he had felt tired. It seemed to annoy him I even asked.

And then, sitting close to Willie so often, I noticed he smelled. Not dirty, but sweet, a strange sort of sweet, not nice. Manang had said sometimes bad spirits went to live right inside people. I didn't know why the smell made me remember that. It scared me a little. I asked Willie about the smell in a jokey way, but his whole face tightened up. "Piss off!" he said. He was so furious he trembled. "Just piss off!" he hissed. And after that day Willie found excuses: he was too tired; he was too busy to work with me. He wrapped his silence around him; I had no weapon against it. I wanted my friend back, I liked his world, but it was no use. I had let him down.

About this time it was decided—by my mother, Mrs Crone, and a few other women—that I was big enough to do more around the house. I already swept the hallway and front steps daily; now, my mother said, in rotation with some other children, I was to keep the toilet clean. The toilet was a shame, she said— diarrhea, far too many people using it, some of them unhandy little kids, and maybe some unhandy adults too. Lately, she added, the little room seemed messier than ever; nobody knew why. The walls had pee on them, even smears. I was to inspect regularly, every day, for a week, and use a mop when needed.

I didn't mind. It was a real job, not just a chore such as sweeping. I got there early before the morning rush and straightaway afterwards. Then the windowless little room stank, but not so bad—nothing like Peter under his sheet or the boar's head in the ground. I stopped in at mid-morning, noon, mid-afternoon, after adults returned from work, and before I went to bed. Like a policeman, I stood in line just to check up. Duty undid my own routines, of course, and they were cut short and rescheduled. I missed Willie a little less.

It helped me enormously that first week on the job when Mrs Crone pinned to the wall above the toilet a long poem about shitting. Mrs Crone would say of herself: "I'm not a figure who remains in the shadow." And one way she came out of the shadow was to write stinging or loving or funny lines that rhymed, on any subject. Young and old, small and big, rich and poor, we all have to shit, said the poem, or we die. It went on and on in very correct Dutch except that every line began with the word shit. Finally, it asked the reader, please, to shit properly, to aim true. After two days, when everyone in the house who could read had to have read it, Mrs Crone took the poem down. Months later, though, she could still recite it from memory for my pleasure.

I kept the toilet very clean and adults praised me, which, unlike Willie, I enjoyed. But something was happening there. While mopping, I had the door wide open to let daylight in; usually you sat there with the room lit only by a tiny bulb on the ceiling. Every day, a different spot on one of the toilet's white-painted walls, near the floor, high up, anywhere, was slightly darkened with moisture. Old blots had turned faintly yellow. Worse, here and there, always high up, were small smirches. I couldn't believe it—somebody was dirtying up the toilet on purpose. If I told my mother, what could she do? It could be anybody. There were forty or more people who used the toilet; how would she figure out who it was? Jerry, the same thing; and he might insist we let the adults know. There'd be a terrible ruckus. Mrs Crone might write another poem. Mrs Slierendrecht might have a fit. Ankie? No, I couldn't tell Ankie: her face might close.

I would keep quiet. It was, after all, my toilet that week; and I'd ask, beg even, that they let me take care of it the next week, too. I would wash the walls—not so difficult—and then check for fresh stains; what puzzled me was the spread of the pee marks: how was it done? I would find out. I would hide in a cluster of bushes near the bathroom and the toilet—and watch everybody going in and out. I would join many line-ups. I would look in on the toilet late at night. It could be fun. In time the patient, cunning watcher would run the guilty one to earth. It would be like hunting.

Some people, of course, were definitely innocent. My mother and Jerry, the Crones, Willie and his mother and sister, the Slierendrechts—well, maybe not Mrs Slierendrecht; also, really little kids couldn't have reached the height of the smudges. That still left quite a few suspects though.

And then, when I knew who it was, what would I do? If I told my mother she would perhaps talk quietly with the person; but she also might first want to discuss it with Mrs Crone who didn't like staying in the shadow—and there could be a row. There had to be something wrong with whoever filthied up a toilet on purpose. It was sort of sad. I thought about Dirk long ago cheating over soldiers. Also sad, and bad—and what had my mother answered when I asked how I could help him? Just stay yourself, she'd said.

I knew what to do. I'd write a note. I couldn't write very well, but I'd fox the spelling of the words out of Jerry and then, when I was sure who it was, I would slip the paper to him or her without letting on, of course, that it came from me. The note would say: STOP IT IN THE TOILET.

The toilet was now spotless. I stood in line, made sudden visits, crouched in the bushes watching: some people went often. On the seventh day, about three in the afternoon when it was still and very hot, I saw Willie go in and as he came out again he was stuffing something into his pants pocket. I went into the toilet and there was a wet patch at about the height of my head. I wiped it off.

I went to our room and lay down by the window. It must have been a little can or cup in Willie's pocket. There was one Willie, I thought, a quiet, kind boy who sat hunched over his table hour after hour healing watches. And then there was another who was mad because he had to wear a hat, suddenly needed rest, and lived in a skin that smelled sweet. Was the second Willie so angry, so angry and helpless, that all he could do was, in a half-dark toilet, foul up the walls with his pee and shit? Would I have? I'd never had such an anger. Maybe I would.

I wrote no note. I never told anyone. I just cleaned up after Willie and he must have noticed because before my second week was done he'd stopped. One day, he and his family packed and moved out of our neighbourhood. His mother told someone that a person had died and a nice room had come free.

EIGHT / Ankie

ANKIE CRONE was a mystery. Of course, when I thought about it, everybody was a mystery in a way, even my mother and Jerry. You felt you knew just who a person was, had come to their "end," and then he or she did or said something completely unexpected. But the mystery of Ankie was different again. What it was, I didn't understand. When our lives later moved apart I stopped thinking about the mystery and I stopped thinking about Ankie, although I never forgot her.

On the first day in Tjihapit Ankie had knocked on our door while my mother was still fixing up the new room. She stuck her head in and said she just wanted to say hello and offered tea: neighbourliness was not so common any more. She told us her name and my mother told her ours and said come in. Ankie looked around the room, at every small adornment, the drawings, the flowers, the leaves, and smiled with pleasure. *"Wat gezellig!"* she said. *Gezellig* means cozy, comfortable, homey, friendly, cheerful, snug, festive, hearty, and more; it's an important Dutch word. She confessed her family's room wasn't very *gezellig*. I stared at her. Brown hair fell curling inward to just above slender shoulders. The skin looked baby-soft. The voice was faintly nasal. It was the smile, though, where the mystery began for me: her whole face smiled and she gave that small moan.

Ankie would go back to her family's room and also set out cans and bottles with flowers and leaves; she would find pictures to pin up, cloths to drape. What's more, I thought she came to really appreciate my mother, as did Mrs Crone: value her common sense and lack of self-pity, and enjoy her odd Dutch. I knew this, because Ankie told me so. "Your mother is an example to me," she said once, "and always will be."

It was new to have someone older talk to me seriously, even if only about my mother. In and around the house I grew alert to Ankie's whereabouts and doings. I always first thought what to ask or tell her and then about how she might react. I didn't mind her face closing—all her faces were fine—as long as it wasn't because I had said something childish or ugly or had interrupted her sitting alone on the front steps staring. I didn't come near after overhearing an argument in her family's room, or, of course, if Polo was around. I stayed away when the Japanese said that boys of Harry's and Polo's age had become "a danger to the state" and the next day trucked them out of Tjihapit to nobody knew where. Driving out of the camp gate, many of those big boys waving goodbye were smiling: it was an adventure. I also never forgot that Ankie was older—she had breasts—and that to her I was a little boy. So I was careful approaching her and kept visits short. Mostly we just chatted, her thoughts, I could tell, often straying. The trick for me was to grow beyond cute and sweet to interesting. Now and then it worked and at such moments I briefly felt hot with certainty that her attention was fully on me. Many times, I wouldn't have minded not saying a word. I just wanted to be near her.

Sunlight showed up tiny blonde hairs on her forearms. On the front steps she'd sit down, cross her legs, wriggle for comfort, straighten her skirt, and start to swing a foot, and I'd wish she'd get up and do it all again. It was always the same finger that hooked her hair from her eyes. Her mouth looked so soft. The small, quick, busy hands also sometimes lay as if asleep in her lap. Standing up and bending over, her bum stuck out. She hummed a lot. Excitement set off red blotches on her cheeks. When she stretched to hang up washing, her shadow fell slim and curved like young bamboo. Her skin was light pink from the throat down, and on, I supposed. Her voice could soothe like falling water. She wore lipstick on special occasions. If she sat very still I could see her breathing. The eyes, troubled often, were older than she was. When she squatted to pick flowers she tucked her skirt deep between her thighs. She smelled of herself and of laundry soap. Her speaking was sprinkled with "umms" and "ahhs." When she touched me, even by chance, the feel lingered. Sometimes, when happy, she'd run around in long dance jumps. She walked with the sway of a woman. She was a promise.

Across the street, in a house as crowded as ours, there lived a mother and two children, a girl and a boy, about two and five, all with fiery red hair. Sometimes, sitting on our front steps, Ankie and I watched them. Small and muscled, the mother had her hair cut very short and she had a terrible temper. One moment she'd be quietly wandering around their yard, carrying the girl, holding the boy's hand, and in the next the girl had been plunked down crying and the mother was yelling at the boy, shaking a finger in his face. Then the mother would snatch up the girl and, still shouting, grab the boy by the arm and drag him into the house.

It wasn't unusual to see women blow up at their children, or at each other: camp life was dreary but always charged because

torment never let up. Just to pester prisoners, a neighbourhood's water or electricity might without warning be cut off for
a day or two. A promised truckload of bananas wouldn't arrive.
A sugar ration was held back. Soldiers might suddenly burst
barking into a house, order everyone out, and ransack it
searching for, say, scissors and knives—and so pettily fixed were
they then on just those items that they'd miss or ignore any
other contraband. And always there were bans: all velos and
tanks forbidden; no more religious services; all team sports,
such as soccer, prohibited; and, of course, strictly no *gedekken*.
Gedekken drove them mad; shaving a smuggler's head repre-
sented chopping it off with a samurai sword. Over time, though,
prisoners' flare-ups slackened: there was no energy.

We got used to the redhead's scenes, but then they began
to change. The mother worked and the boy was left in charge of
his sister; it couldn't have left him much time to play. She'd
come home and later the three of them would go out into the
garden. They had a vegetable plot and she and the boy watered
and weeded as the girl sat and looked on. The boy seemed to
make mistakes or was slow. First she just screamed at him—but
then he started to scream back. She would whack him on his
behind. He'd run away, she'd catch him, they'd struggle, and
the girl sitting in the grass might burst into tears. No one inter-
fered. From that the sessions grew, day by day, to the mother
hitting the boy in the face with her open hand while he tried to
fight back, to pushing and hitting him until he fell, to finally
going at him with her fists and bare feet, just beating and
kicking him, screeching that he was a rotten child, a filthy child,
a dog.

One day, sitting on our front steps, Ankie said, "That's
enough." She got up and crossed the road. I trailed behind. Was

she going to fight the mother? Ankie once told me about a boy named Hans who had suddenly given her a kiss, her first, on her cheek, and she had slapped his face. She was soft but there was a limit. The woman now had the boy by the shoulders and was shaking and shaking him so his head flopped around; veins stood out in her neck. Gently, politely, Ankie called the mother's name. Dropping the boy, she swung around; he scurried to where his sister was sitting. The woman stood with her hands in her sides, breathing hard, not saying anything; she wasn't much bigger than Ankie but a lot stronger. Ankie had her hands clasped behind her and she took a few small steps closer. I stayed where I was. In that same voice Ankie said, "I wondered about something—if you have time?" Then she was standing by the mother, finger tips on her arm, murmuring. She pointed to the vegetable bed, moved towards it. The woman stood like a rock at first, then her arms fell, she gave me a look, and she let Ankie steer her away.

I walked backwards to our front steps. First they bent over the vegetable bed, then they knelt by it. The boy had disappeared. Ankie and the woman got up and sat with the girl, played with her. There was a real conversation going.

Maybe half an hour later Ankie came back across. What had she said to the woman, I wanted to know. "I asked about lettuce." But what about the boy, the beatings? She hadn't mentioned him or them. She said she and the woman had talked about his sister and then about themselves as little girls. They had laughed about what an awful lot you can remember from when you were small. Ankie was beginning to stare, her eyes older: I should leave.

The redhead's flare-ups didn't stop altogether—she had a temper—but I didn't see her hit her son again.

The red tile roof of our house hung over so far that in the rain you could sit on the two top front steps and stay dry. Rain came down with the same force as on the plantation, but there you could often see it coming. In Bandung, which lies in a valley, the dark clouds sneaked up from behind the mountains and streaked down to burst apart over the city; in the wet season almost every afternoon, long driving gushes. Streets steamed, sewers gargled, and plants hugged the ground. Those rains could quickly turn gardens into swamps and parts of streets into streams; their drum and clatter, as always, shrank the world.

Ankie, being older, heard more news than I. When I was sitting on the front steps with her once watching the rain, she told me that on the other side of the camp a young Indonesian had tossed a bunch of bananas over the wall to a woman, not to trade, but out of *kasihan*, pity.

She hunched her shoulders as if cold.

The Japanese had spotted the man, she went on, thrashed him, then stood him up in the street where he'd thrown the fruit with a sign around his neck saying, "I gave bananas to the rotten Dutch." He was to stand there for six days without food and water. Late at night women waited for the guard to grow sleepy and then somehow passed food and drink to the young man, and he lived.

The man with the sign must have felt very alone, I said to Ankie, especially in the dark.

Yes, she said, very.

To be alone in the dark was the worst, I said.

She nodded.

There were rumours that soon boys even of Jerry's age were going to be picked up because they were a "danger to the state."

She'd heard that, too.

85

Jerry would drive out of the camp in a truck like Harry and Polo—and then I wouldn't have a brother any more. My brother would be gone. I wouldn't know where he was or whether he was dead or alive. Sometimes, when I woke in the night, I told her, I climbed over my mother asleep and looked out our window at the stars. Manang, our gardener, had not mentioned spirits living on the stars but I thought they probably did. They had to be lonely so far from the world. On earth, spirits had us at least.

Ankie looked up at the rain. If she went out into it she would look as she did after a bath, her hair clinging flat to her neck, ears, and sides of her face—fresh, like the girl sitting by the holy banyan tree watching the trucks.

And, of course, I said, we had the spirits. If you got really lonely you could think about the spirits all around you, as Manang was positive they were—well, that might make you feel better. But what if Jerry went away? Would thinking about spirits help then? Also, my mother might die. She had a lot of common sense but it could happen, people died all the time. The women who made coffins had to work hard. If my mother died I'd be completely alone and knowing there were lots of spirits around, well, I didn't think it would cheer me up. No, because I wouldn't have my mother. She would be gone.

I had Ankie's attention.

That was the trouble these days, I told her, you didn't get to keep what you had. Nobody. Nothing. The plantation, my father, Manang, Mr Otten, Uncle Fred, Jerry's bike, my iron collection, Leo, Mr Plomp—gone. The boar's head—gone. Bloemenkamp, Dirk, my yellow kite, Mrs Plomp, Mrs Witte—gone. Peter in the hospital—gone; dead probably. And now perhaps Jerry. If this kept up there'd be nobody and nothing left.

She was still listening.

She knew, of course, that Jesus had said "Love your enemy"? Yes.

Well now, how could anybody—anybody—love the damn Japs? They took away everybody and everything. They were thieves.

It was still pouring. Ankie got up, stretched. I watched her from her toes on up—she looked so smooth all her clothes had to be made of silk. She frowned. She would have to think about that, she said, and went inside.

Another time, maybe also on the front steps in the rain, I brought up Manang again, his squatting all the time, the guns and knives he carved, and the cowardly spirit living inside that made him so afraid of Leo. We talked about fear. That day Ankie was wearing glasses for the first time, rimless: they made her small eyes larger.

There were different kinds of fear, Ankie said. Before we had come to live in Tjihapit, she told me, one night a woman had swapped a pair of pyjama pants at the wall for twelve hard-boiled duck eggs. After she had her eggs she threw up the pants and ran; the pants, though, snagged on top of the wall. The Indonesian outside was trying to free them with a stick when he was caught. The Japanese beat the man until he had to be dragged away. By then it was light and the entire camp was ordered out on a field. An officer yelled for the *gedekker* to come forward. Nobody moved. You will all stand here until she does, he screamed, and marched off. Soldiers with rifles with bayonets kept watch and the camp stood in the sun all morning and all afternoon. People fainted. Children cried.

Ankie shivered. She said the air had been full of fear. People feared for themselves, for their children, for their mothers, for the old, and for the sick. They knew that the officer would let them stand and stand—for days—if the smuggler wasn't found. He would never let them go; whoever had the eggs must be found or he would "lose face." People were going to die on that field. It was towards evening that someone told a soldier who the *gedekker* was. He barked for her to come to him, while another soldier trotted off to fetch the officer. Ankie knew the woman slightly: her name was Loes and she was thirty-seven years old. Ankie was standing nearby when the officer came. He didn't shout at the woman or hit her. He took her by the elbow and leading her away he said quietly in Indonesian, "Too bad, Miss Loes."

What I was afraid of, I told Ankie, was that we would always be prisoners.

No, one day we'll be free, she said.

I didn't think so. The Japanese held us, I said, and they weren't going to let us go. Otherwise, why hadn't they done so already? Why had they even picked up women and children? We weren't men, we couldn't fight them. No, they kept us in camps because they liked it. They hated us. We were the enemy. We were being punished because they thought we were bad, and they were going to keep on punishing us. They would always think we were bad; we would never leave the camp. Without hope we die, Ankie murmured.

On the plantation I was able to see so far, I told her, and it was green and quiet. Here the wall stopped your eyes, and there were always other people around. I felt cramped.

Ankie nodded. She was leaning forward, hands under her jaw, elbows on her thighs, legs stretched.

I said the Japanese must think we were getting worse because there was less food all the time and more punishment.

A woman who hadn't bowed properly was made to kneel on a gravel path for four hours. In Japanese eyes we must be so bad. Maybe we were.

She shook her head no. Raindrops spattered her bare feet. She turned. I had her attention.

I was an idiot, she said quietly. This was a war—and the Japanese had started it. Now they were fighting us and the Americans and the English, almost everybody, except the Germans and Italians. We were in camp and being starved and hurt because that's how they fought a war. We were victims. None of us were bad. Not me either. I was an idiot, she smiled, to think that maybe I was bad, that maybe I was guilty.

From crashing down, the rain was now just falling steadily.

It was the Japanese who were guilty, she said, her cheeks red. And one day they would pay for it.

What was "guilty," I asked.

If you did something wrong you were guilty, at fault, to blame, for having done it, Ankie said.

I thought that over. And then I said that for a while now I had been feeling guilty about just about everything.

She waited.

I wanted to tell her about Willie and his toilet messes. Sure they had been his, but just the same I felt guilty about them. I didn't have Willie's anger that made him a little crazy—only he had it. Was that fair? But I kept quiet about Willie. Instead I told her about Peter in the hospital stinking under his sheet. It was long ago, but I could still see the huge eyes in the white face. The pain from his smashed leg had been a hundred times worse than mine from my finger. Was that fair? He shouldn't have suffered so much. And damn, why hadn't I had my harmonica with me to give him?

Ankie had a tiny approving smile for this—as I knew she would. I really had wanted Peter to have the harmonica though.

But I also felt guilty, I said, about the woman Loes and all those people afraid on the field, even whoever had told on Loes, and the woman on the gravel, the Indonesian with the sign around his neck, the coffins being carried out the camp gate, my Aunt Ina in hospital again, Dirk the cheat, my mother's thinness, Jerry maybe leaving, everything. Inside small coffins were dead children. The smallest coffins held babies who must have gone straight from being born to being dead. My father had said religion was nonsense. Well, God was letting it happen, wasn't He? It made me tired.

Ankie was looking down at her wet feet. She sighed, lightly lifting the swellings inside her blouse. She was very serious. She said she thought that perhaps many people felt this guilt. She did sometimes. But she was sure it wasn't right. She touched my forehead. I had to think it away, she said.

I trusted Ankie. I tried.

Anna Hillen with her sons, Ernest, aged one, and Jerry, aged five, at home in Scheveningen, Holland

John and Anne Hillen reading with their sons at home in Holland, 1936

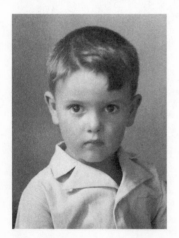

Ernest at about age three

John Hillen, Jerry, and Ernest on the tea planta-tion in the mountains about Bandung, Java

Father and sons watching Indonesians playing soccer on the field below

Anna and John Hillen
in the lush garden of
the plantation,
September 1938

Jerry reading out loud to Ernest, 1938:
"Jerry was my best friend"

A visiting tukang tjukur *at work on Jerry; and the final result of the barber's efforts*

"What Jerry really liked was to be alone and read"

Anna Hillen and her sons on the front steps of the plantation's main house, 1937

Aerial photograph of the tea plantation, showing the factory, the swimming pool, and the Hillen home (top right), 1939

Ernest, Jerry, and Ineke and Hanneke Staal: "They were like our sisters; all four of us had brown eyes"

Ernest, Hanneke, Jerry, and Ineke, 1939: "Every day held the certainty of play in the pool. It was never denied"

Anna shopping in the market, 1939

The last picture the family in Holland received from Anna, September 1940

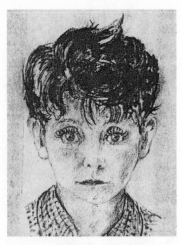

Left: *A drawing of Ernest, 1944: "Events and people that would stir me were like little flames that camp life quickly dimmed or smothered"*;
Right: *A drawing of Corry Vonk by fellow prisoner Pam Ingenegeren, 1944: "She had magic inside her. Up close she sparked"*

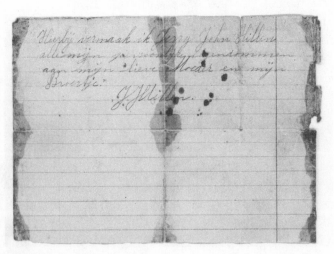

What Jerry wrote when he had to leave his mother and borther in 1943: "Herewith, I, Jerry John Hillen, bequeath all my personal possessions to my dear mother and my Little Brother. J.J. Hillen" (translated from the Dutch)

Left: Ankie, 1945: "Ankie had a way of speaking and smiling at the same time"; Right: Zuseke Crone: "I thought her face should be carved in stone"

A photograph that appeared in the Toronto Star, *March 21, 1946, upon mother and sons' safe arrival in Canada*

Ernest in Canada, aged twelve: "Memory is, finally, all we own"

NINE / Jerry

WE MUST HAVE LOOKED as if we were celebrating—sitting
cross-legged on the "living-room" mattress, talking low, laughing,
nibbling treats. From somewhere our mother had scrounged a
few bananas and oranges and a bowl of the milk and scraped-out
flesh of a young coconut; earlier Mrs Crone had handed a saucer
of homemade palm-sugar fudge around the door. The window
was shuttered, the one lamp covered with black cloth. The
Japanese hated the dark, were scared of it some said, and at night
kept their own quarters ablaze while forever badgering us to save
electricity. Lights out at eight was the rule—one of the few my
mother ever broke. She read as late as she pleased, if she had a
book and wasn't too tired; it was at this time that she was copying
out *The Hermit*. What light there was fell at the head end of her
mattress where she was folding clothes and stuffing them into a
rucksack; a little suitcase stood ready by the door.

The awful rumour had come true: boys of Jerry's age,
thirteen-year-olds, were a definite "danger to the state" to be
trucked away to no one knew where. To stir up panic the
Japanese had told the camp only at midday that the boys were
to report at the gate next morning at six. They seemed afraid of
young boys because some months later there would be a call-
up of twelve-year-olds, then eleven-year-olds, which I just
missed; ten-year-olds would have been next if the war had gone

on. The lower the cut-off age fell, the harder wailed the frantic mothers bunched at camp gates seeing their children hauled away. Once a group of them dared to protest, and were beaten and locked up.

Our mother's lips had grown thin on hearing the news, but then, as expected, she told Jerry it was an adventure, his biggest—and on his own. We stayed up late that night, which didn't matter because my brother had a clock inside that woke him when he told it to. I tried to see his face in the dark. Some people found Jerry dull because he was quiet and seemed shy, but those soft brown eyes could blaze with pain or fun. He read whenever and whatever he could and, like Ankie, would sit still and stare. He wouldn't say what was in his head then; they weren't secret thoughts, he'd explain, just private. I felt they might be a little sad because often that's how his eyes looked. I had overheard our mother say about him that he was "deep." I was the one who made grown-ups laugh. Jerry had no special friends and was alone a lot. When he played it was mostly with me—but no real-fighting games. We never needed to say much; he seemed to feel safe then and even laughed out loud. The age gap still made no difference, except that I got my way a lot. We were as one against outsiders, and never told on each other: that was dishonourable. On his time off we still roamed through the stinking sewer alleys looking for stuff, silent as Indians.

In the dark room I could make out Jerry's shape and the whites of his eyes. He stood up and shuffled this way and that on the mattress, hands in his pockets, saying out loud, it seemed, whatever came into his mind. On the plantation one night he had spied in his pyjamas on the adults playing Monopoly—our parents and Uncle Fred and Aunt Ina. Our parents and Uncle Fred laughed more and more, Jerry said, as a flustered Aunt Ina turned more glum. After a bit he realized the three had ganged up on her and were cheating. He'd started to giggle and had to scramble away.

What an imagination, murmured our mother.

Always calm and gentle and friendly was how Jerry remembered Uncle Fred. He thought Aunt Ina, on the other hand, was usually tense and strict and prickly.

If you can't say something nice about a person, say nothing; our mother slipped an always-useful tea towel into the backpack. But she'd more than once called Uncle Fred "an example of a fine man" and I thought she liked him a lot.

Turning to me, Jerry said that during a New Year's celebration, I'd held a lit firecracker behind my ear to find out just how loud it sounded and after the bang had burst into tears.

Never, I hissed.

Jerry flopped down full length on the mattress. The first book he had ever read was *Robinson Crusoe*. On the plantation he remembered fire-red hibiscus with metal-green leaves and grass so lush it had looked good enough to eat. Why, by the way, he asked our mother, did she never wear trousers?

She felt more womanly in a dress, she said.

Jerry rolled back and forth. He had seen one film in his life, *Snow White and the Seven Dwarfs*, in Bandung; I had been too young to go. Our mother remembered a huge Snow White jigsaw puzzle he had assembled on the dining-room table. In Bloemenkamp, while working in the kitchen, Jerry told us he had seen a soldier beat an older boy with a piece of firewood gripped in both hands. He missed Bloemenkamp: it now seemed almost luxurious—quieter, more to eat, lighter work. Our mother had roasted peanuts there that he sold door to door so we'd have extra money—one egg-cup full for one cent;

the Dutch pennies had holes in the centre and he had threaded them on a shoelace with a knot on the end.

Jerry suddenly asked for paper and a pen. Our mother dug a scrap out of her purse and a short pencil. Jerry said a pencil would fade. Sorry, she didn't have a pen. He crawled over to the light and she shifted to make room. Lying on his stomach he held the paper down on *The Hermit* and began to write slowly. My mother and I waited. Then he scrawled his signature, fast like our father did, folded the paper twice, and tucked it and the pencil back into the purse. As if he were an adult, in that tone of voice, he told our mother that we were forbidden to read it until he was gone.

The word "gone" echoed a little, but Jerry wouldn't let it change the mood. After writing his note, he was a little bit in charge. He jumped to the end of the mattress where I was sitting and yanked me up. "Those breasts at the pool on the plantation were pointy, *pointy*," he breathed into my ear (with our mother right there!). "From the cold water," he finished in a normal voice.

What cold water, our mother wanted to know.

But by then Jerry had me in a neck hold and was dragging me across the mattress. He was never the one to start, didn't like it—but I loved wrestling. We fought on, puffing and snorting. Our mother sat by the lamp hugging her knees, rocking herself. We rolled and twisted and leg-pressed the air out of each other. I felt I was beginning to win, but I almost always did with Jerry. He wriggled free and rolled towards our mother. There were three pieces of fudge left on the saucer.

We should eat those, he said, and then we'd better go to bed. Our mother agreed, and lightly held his chin a moment.

But on our side of the room, Jerry wasn't ready for sleep yet. He asked if I remembered Itjeh. I didn't much: she was our cook on the plantation and had a mouth stained red from chewing *sirih*, betel nut. One day, he whispered, Itjeh's husband came to say she couldn't work because she was sick. Jerry decided to visit her; he'd done so before. In front of her one-room bamboo hut on stilts he called "Itjeh!" and she answered from inside to come in. There was a bucket of water by the steps and he first washed his feet. When he opened the door he could just see her half-sitting up in the smoky dimness wrapped in a sarong on a sleeping mat; a child lay asleep nearby. She thanked him for coming, but really she would be fine, she said; she would cook again tomorrow. He took a step closer to see better. But you're sick, he said. No, not sick, she smiled with red teeth. What is wrong with you then, Itjeh, Jerry said sternly. "Oh, you good boy," Itjeh laughed, "it is only this," and from behind her she lifted a cloth soaked with blood. Jerry shot out of the door and down the steps. He ran home and into our house yelling that Itjeh was bleeding to death, that she was dying, dying.

I'd never heard this story and waited for the end, but that was it. Jerry said no more. Why tell half, I wondered to myself, getting sleepy.

I turned and asked in his ear if he was scared about tomorrow. No, he said.

On the plantation, he mumbled after a moment, he had liked playing soccer because the Indonesian boys always let him be goalkeeper.

Jerry had set his inside clock early and was already washed and dressed when he woke us. Our mother pushed open the shutters. Grey light showed mist clinging to the ground and a fine drizzle. No cock had cried yet. We heard stumbles next door: the Crones had said they'd come to the gate; Ineke and Hanneke, too. Aunt Ina and Erik were sick. As our mother and I dressed, Jerry swung the backpack on and off his shoulders whistling to himself; the hole his lips formed was never in the centre of his mouth but to the right, giving him a crooked look. We ate small hunks of the glue-like bread and drank water, my brother standing by the door, rucksack on his back.

Once out in the light rain, Jerry began to march, swinging the suitcase, chin up, straight as a soldier. Our mother kept up but I had to trot. I was going to dash forward and imitate him, but it suddenly didn't seem funny. I trudged on behind. From side streets and lanes small solemn groups with a boy at the centre turned onto the main road to the gate. Some women and girls were already crying. I ran to check our mother; but, no, she was calmly stepping at the same pace as Jerry. I slowed down. Puddles were forming, nice to stomp in, but that was too childish this grey-drab morning. That was my brother up ahead, my only brother, going away. In minutes my mother and I would be walking back, without him. He would be on a truck off to no one knew where. He would be gone. Just gone. I tried to imagine it. But he had always been there, always. He was there now, striding along in front of me—brave. He had been brave with Leo, that crazy dog, and now he was brave again, like a man almost. I was nearly crying, but I didn't: Jerry and our mother didn't cry. Damnit, though, he was supposed to stay. He had painted his bike for me, invented invisible girls, shot me in the eye, fought for me, made me a kite, hunted and boxed and swum and smoked with me; together we had mowed down enemy soldiers and pretended to be horses; he had read to me and listened to my Chinese-girl stories. He was the one who had put his arm around me when I had my wound, told me about breasts, and built me a tank. He shouldn't leave me. I was his brother.

At the gate ahead soldiers were herding boys into a line-up behind a truck while others held back family and friends with their rifles. Clothes stuck to bodies and faces shone wetly in the rain. The calling and sobbing by mothers and sisters swelled to loud, raw crying. Two officers holding umbrellas, their flat black gaze missing nothing, flanked a camp-office woman who shouted numbers from a list. As boys responded, soldiers hustled them onto the truck—*Lekas! Lekas!* "Hurry! Hurry!"

The Crones pushed their way through to us and quickly hugged Jerry, and so did Ineke and Hanneke. My mother took his face between her hands and kissed each cheek. They said something to each other that I couldn't hear. Then Jerry gripped my hand, looked me in the eyes, and, like our father had done when he left, said, "Take care of Mom." He freed his hand and knuckle-rapped me on the head. "Don't play *litjik*," he smiled, meaning "false" in Indonesian, and turned and ran for the line-up.

We stayed in place. Mrs Crone put her arm around my mother. The tailboard of the first truck was slammed shut; standing pressed together, the boys waved, some crying, most not. Mothers clawed the air and screamed and surged against the hard rifles. As the truck rumbled out of the gate, a second one hastily backed in, its engine left running. Boys were hoisted into the back with speed. I couldn't spot Jerry at first but then he was clambering up, too, one of the last. He stood on his toes, his eyes searching for us—and he was grinning. Why the hell was he grinning? When he saw us he swung his hands in fists above his head as if he'd won a race; then he just looked. For a second I was inside him, looking over the wet heads of the crowd sealing in the faces of mother and brother, the truck's floor shuddering beneath bare feet. Bolts clanged, gears screaked, and the truck moved off. We waved with two arms, and so did Jerry. He was grinning again. Through the gate, the truck turned sharply right and out of sight behind the bamboo fence. He was gone.

All the way home my mother walked with her hand resting on my shoulder. The Crones and Ineke and Hanneke had stayed to watch the last truck leave. Why, I wanted to know immediately, had he been grinning. Excitement, my mother said, and feeling happy. But wasn't it sad leaving us? Yes, she said, and tonight, wherever he might be, he would be very lonely. But this was also a huge adventure: for the first time Jerry would be his own boss, and that was a great feeling. I didn't bother to imagine her ever not being her own boss. Not only that, she said, but Jerry, who was usually alone when he wasn't with us, was now one of that group of boys; he belonged. She and I would talk about him, she said, just as we talked about my father and his mother and Uncle Fred and her father and mother and grandfather and sister, Ada, and dead sister, Helen, and brother, Alfred, who also had red hair and freckles.

At home our room looked empty. Before she went to work, my mother pulled the folded piece of paper out of her purse. Jerry had written in Dutch: "Herewith I Jerry John Hillen bequeath all my personal belongings to my dear Mother and my little Brother."

Most of that day I stayed in our room lying on my mother's mattress beneath the window. I felt tired. I tried to think about Jerry but it just hurt; it was as if something of myself was gone.

Wherever he was, at least there would be spirits around him, even now on the truck, though they would be asleep because it was daytime; but at night they would sit on the roof under which he was sleeping and in the treetops all around. They would keep an eye on him.

"He was my best friend, you know," I said that evening when my mother kissed me good-night. "I'll never have such a friend again."

"You will so," she whispered, "you'll see."

I wanted to believe her, but I didn't really. Jerry was gone.

About half a year later, or maybe it was a year later, we got a postcard from Jerry in Indonesian in block letters, one of three postcards we would receive in total. Besides the required sentences—such as, "We have plenty of food and much recreation" or "The Japanese treat us well so don't worry about me"—the sender had twenty-five "free" words. Into those words Jerry had worked "Baptista," my father's middle name. That told us they were in the same camp. It made my mother very happy. She told everybody: father and son, mother and son—how lucky we were. I was glad, too, of course, that Jerry was safe. But I also knew then that he was certainly not his own boss and that he would be taught a lot of discipline.

TEN / Corry Vonk

HEROES WERE ALWAYS MEN; all the stories I'd heard said so. The one exception was my own Chinese girl who roamed the countryside without fear in red boots and once fought off a python by pressing her fingers into its nose holes until it fainted. It was men who were brave, clever, wise, proud, and saved everybody. Women were usually helpless and weak, but good at having babies and bandaging wounds. Heroes protected women but didn't take them seriously, unless they were "in love," and then briefly. Women were, or were not, kind, gently strong, and soothing. Women, though, were not heroes. To me this was so. But it has to be said that I was wrong. Tjihapit held no hunters, pilots, cowboys, or Indians, but just the same a couple of real heroes lived there—and they were both women. Maybe my mother was a hero, too, but she was my mother.

Heat, hunger, and the sameness of life in camp, made you slow, even a little stupid, and it took me a while to recognize the first hero. Like a naughty, clownish puppet with huge blue eyes that could suddenly fill with tears, she was not much taller than me and as thin. Her dark-brown hair with three or four silver streaks running through was cut short as a boy's, her large mouth lipsticked deep red, with round touches of it on her cheeks, and her eyelashes thickly blackened. It was a mask. A hundred masks really, because she could, and did, pull her face every which way from grief to delight to shock to innocence. It made people laugh. And they laughed at what she said in her husky strong voice, surprising from someone so small, in exaggerated foreign accents, in high and low Dutch, and in tones from command to snivelling. Sometimes she shocked people a bit, but it was hard not to laugh when you were near her. I was in the same camps with Corry Vonk until the end, and that's what she did: she made us laugh.

Corry Vonk was the wife of Wim Kan and both were cabaret stars. They had gotten stuck on a tour in Indonesia when the Germans invaded Holland. After the Japanese won, Mr Kan was shipped off to a camp in Burma. Mrs Kan-Vonk landed in Tjihapit and at once wangled permission from the Japanese to set up a cabaret by and for prisoners. It was called *Les deux ânes,* "The Two Donkeys," and she ran it with a blonde-haired friend named Puk Meijer. The camp's commandant even gave Corry Vonk a title: *Hanchó main main, Hanchó* meaning "boss" in Japanese, and *main main,* "play" in Indonesian.

When we moved into Tjihapit, Corry Vonk and her friend lived next door in a garage. Corry Vonk was slight, noisy, and wore bright cloth twisted into scarfs and belts; Puk Meijer was heavy, quiet, and dressed darkly; both were usually in trousers. Each morning they thrust the garage doors wide apart as if opening a store. In the rear behind a sheet-curtain lay their two mattresses and on nails along the three walls hung unusual clothes and hats, tennis rackets, a broken telephone, an outsize frying pan, beards, all sorts of odd things, and, on a nail by itself, dark-brown and ragged, the camp's only wig. Young women dropped by and sat on the floor sewing costumes, or stood around singing or shouting dialogue at each other. Corry

Vonk, in her blunt way, made them repeat the songs and lines over and over and over again. In the afternoon she'd march off to work and the garage would grow quiet.

In an abandoned house, with help from volunteers, the two had knocked down walls so a hundred and fifty women and children could crowd together on the "theatre" floor, and built a stage out of bamboo, chicken wire, old sheets, and coloured rags; from somewhere an old piano had been carted in. The entry fee was one guilder and the proceeds went to poor women or to the camp hospital for medicine and extra food. (At first, people in the camps still had a little money and certain supplies could be bought in the city; later, of course, owning Dutch currency and any dealings with the outside became serious crimes.)

There were always informers in camp—women who for food, cigarettes, light work, and other favours told on the rest of us—so, since Corry Vonk was responsible for every word said on stage, she had to be careful. The Japanese hated criticism, and mockery even more; attention of any sort from them was dangerous, as she very well knew. But with her crazy faces and voices, which were impossible to translate, she was able to make us laugh at the Japanese anyhow, and at ourselves, too.

Still, the authorities didn't make it easy. One day the commandant—who often called for Corry Vonk, perhaps because he too thought she was funny—ordered her to stop charging fees or he'd shut the theatre and punish her. But she seemed to have no fear and she was obstinate. Lookouts were promptly posted so that when spies, most of whom were known to us, showed up at the theatre, cash vanished into deep skirt pockets. Next, the commandant, as a "surprise," had his soldiers build and install a stage backdrop, a huge paper-and-bamboo model of the Japanese holy mountain Fujiyama; he said he was homesick for it. Not to show pleasure would have been insulting, but it looked silly. The commandant invited himself to dress rehearsal and must have been so disappointed at the cast's unreadiness, especially that of three clumsy dancers one of whom misstepped once too often so that her partners tripped, crashed into the mountain, and totally wrecked it.

On another occasion, the commandant told Corry Vonk he'd received a notice from military headquarters in Batavia (Jakarta) banning all religious services, concerts, lectures—and theatrical performances. The story went that she thought hard and fast, pulled her most innocent face, and said that Batavia knew best, of course; it always did. But had Batavia mentioned her acting school and public lessons? The commandant studied the paper on his desk—no, it hadn't. *Hanchó main main's* blue eyes opened wide—well? The commandant frowned, then nodded: if Batavia objected to acting schools and public lessons then Batavia would certainly have said so.

When I met Corry Vonk the first time she didn't say hello: she looked at me, and then slowly winked. It was as if she'd known me a long time and we shared some sort of secret. I winked back. And that's how we greeted each other from then on, me letting her wink first to be polite.

Corry Vonk had magic inside her. Up close she sparked. Always the centre, face and voice never still, she jumped from joke to idea to joke. You'd have thought this would tire people, but it didn't. They laughed; she excited them. And when she pulled a sad face—and it could be really sad—she made you want to cry. Around Corry Vonk others also became funny and had ideas, ideas for the cabaret or for cheering up the poor and sick and punished; for cheering up also meant helping out. She never seemed to let up, whether handing out plucks of hair from the camp's only wig to women who'd been shaved bald to sew onto their headcloths, or begging for money or rice or whatever from those she'd heard had more than the rest. I saw her step up to a woman in the street, a stranger, and fall on her knees, hands up as if praying. The woman couldn't say no, of course, and Corry Vonk blew her a smacking kiss. She mostly got her way, and what she scrounged went to those without. The Japanese now and then handed her gifts of food after the show. This was always shared with the cast, but her own portion seldom got as far as the garage. I knew this because, for a while, I was around her a lot. I thought so much giving away was dumb, though; when I, too, got extra bits of food, I sneaked them home through the sewer alleys, or ate them on the way. But then, Corry Vonk was different. I imagined her late at night on her back on her mattress, whispering jokes and ideas in the dark to Puk Meijer, and then suddenly poking her nose into her pillow and falling instantly asleep like a child.

At first, though, I just watched Corry Vonk and Puk Meijer from the branches of one of the climbable trees in our yard. They were a strange pair: one nervous, always talking; the other steady, reserved. People wondered when, actually, they slept. Running the cabaret meant writing sketches and tunes, finding and fitting costumes, scaring up make-up and props, and endlessly rehearsing amateurs. But they, like the others in the cabaret, had camp duties as well. I didn't know what Puk Meijer did, but Corry Vonk held down one of the few volunteer-only jobs: she washed by hand the hospital's linen and bandages, teeming with the bacteria of every imaginable disease; and towards the end, of course, there was no soap. When I met Corry Vonk in Tjihapit she herself was scurrying around with two tropical ulcers on one of her shins. Many people had them, me too; after dysentery, malaria, and, later, hunger edema, sores were the most common ailment. They could start from a scratch like my wound in Bloemenkamp, fester, and turn into aching pus holes that refused to heal for months. Because of Corry Vonk's long pants, no one could tell, except that she limped a little.

Watching from the tree, I was drawn to the two women, the small one especially. I wasn't shy meeting strangers, but all the activity in that garage was a little unnerving. And then one morning I saw the solid Puk Meijer come from behind their "bedroom" curtain in bare feet wearing white, tight, very short pants. She greeted half a dozen young girls who had been waiting and led them onto the red-earth driveway fronting the garage. In shorts she was a whole other lively, lovely person. There was a spring to her step, and no wonder—Puk Meijer's trousers had hidden the most marvellous, most powerful calves I had ever seen in my life. Massive curves of muscle! I dropped out of the tree and moved nearer.

The girls, thin and barefoot, in shorts, with pinned-up hair, formed a circle around Puk Meijer and did as she did. Hands at her waist, she lifted her chin, and for a moment stood straight and still. Then she slowly raised one leg, toes pointed, stretched it inch by inch forward and up, and unhurriedly let it down again—the standing leg's calf nicely twitching with the strain; and the same with the other leg. Her heavy body looked loose and sure and light. She repeated the movement several times; then again with the legs reaching sideways. Usually so quiet, she kept up a steady patter, coaxing the girls, cheering them on. She joined their circle and showed them how to take long steps like a stork, feet pointed, arms out like wings, hands like butterflies. Round and round they paced under a whitening sun, the skinny girls and the big woman, faster and faster, steps turning into leaps and then into running and flying, like Ankie when she was happy. Hands stuffed in my pockets, I stared from only yards away.

Puk Meijer clapped once and the girls froze. She turned to me and asked smiling if I would like to learn to dance. I said no thank you politely; if only there had been even one boy in the group. The exercises went on. The girls never looked my way again nor did Puk Meijer. After about an hour she clapped twice and the students stood still, flushed and panting, heels touching, feet out in V's. Puk Meijer would now dance alone, a treat for her pupils, I learned, and the way every lesson wound up. For a few minutes, to music only she could hear, spinning and leaping and swaying, her shining-wet body told a little story that ended with her sinking, one leg behind, one in front, right down flat to her crotch, body bent forward as if crushed, wild hair brushing her knee. Then she raised her head and, calves bunched to bursting, slowly drew herself up. The girls applauded and she curtsied to them.

For a while, Puk Meijer, who also performed in the cabaret, held three or four ballet classes a week and I tried to catch them all. By hanging around, I got to know her and Corry Vonk. The two women never really said much to me, but they let me sit on the ramp, or right inside the garage when it rained, and listen and watch and knead my calves. The others who came and went got used to me. The songs and skits they rehearsed I heard so often I learned some by heart. At night I acted them out for my mother, and for Jerry in the beginning when he hadn't left yet—and just like Corry Vonk, I could make them laugh. That was a good feeling, and I would do it again and again, until I was told to shut up.

I asked Corry Vonk if I could come to the theatre with her. She said yes. The most fun was not where the audience sat—I never once saw a performance from there—but in the cramped backstage where in a great muddle women stripped to near nakedness and wrestled their sweating bodies into costumes, and, at two small tables with mirrors, took turns painting their faces, fingers trembling. They were nervous, and giggled and snapped, and ran to the toilet a lot. Mumbling lines, some puffed hard at cigarettes made of straw. Before my eyes, tired, thin women became actresses and dancers, turned beautiful or witchy, or even male. Corry Vonk, the director, had lead roles in nearly every sketch, but it was she who darted around readying and calming the others, often saying, "Don't worry. I'm a professional. You're wonderful."

Through a hole in the curtain I'd watch the room filling up, and heating up: later, every face would gleam. Women and children brought old cushions or stools, or sat on the floor. In the front row were a half-dozen kitchen chairs, always there in case Japanese officers decided to show up. They did, too, though they couldn't have understood much and their faces stayed mostly like stone; but sometimes they laughed when the audience did, and also when it didn't.

The first time backstage I wasn't of any use, unless someone asked for water, so I pressed myself away in corners. The disorder and hurry didn't stop once the show started because between numbers, when the lights were briefly turned off, props had to be switched and people who had several roles, most of all Corry Vonk, needed to change costumes fast. That commotion almost scared me: the actresses weren't jittery any more, but suddenly serious and so alive. By the second performance I knew what to expect, even helped set up props in the dark—and Corry Vonk began giving me a share of her food gifts: at different times I carried home two eggs, some sugar wrapped in banana leaf, and four small green oranges.

I watched from the wings and, especially when Corry Vonk was on, heard the laughter swelling and breaking, swelling and breaking. I now knew that feeling, and wanted it again. One character I especially would like to have played was the one Corry Vonk was famous for herself—a mischievous Amsterdam ragamuffin with a too large, peaked cap over one ear who sometimes sang sorrowful songs. Adults in the audience knew some of the tunes so well they hummed along. I mentioned to Corry Vonk that I had a harmonica. I still knew only a few bars of "Silent Night, Holy Night" but even so hoped I'd be asked to play it in the cabaret. It was all I could think of but she showed no interest.

So I fetched water, lugged props, and waited. I waited through rehearsals and performances of a cabaret version of *Pinocchio*. I waited through the writing of a whole new set of skits. I waited—and then one day Corry Vonk told me I was going to be a boy who had swallowed a *rijksdaalder,* a large silver two-and-a-half-guilder piece. She would play my mother, another woman would be my father, and a third a maid. I was very happy. Sitting at table with my parents I had to pretend to accidentally gulp down the coin hidden in a slice of "cake," then look concerned while the others made a great to-do—and never smile. I had nothing to say. We rehearsed and rehearsed, in the garage, then the theatre. On opening night I was ready early, in shorts, shirt, knee socks, shoes, and red lips. My heart was thumping, but I wasn't scared—until I heard the buzz from the audience coming in. Corry Vonk as usual was everywhere at once. She stopped and looked at me. "You're green," she said in that voice all could hear. "If you need to puke, puke. I'm a pro-fessional. You're wonderful." I did and felt better. On stage I swallowed, looked concerned, and never smiled. I was wonderful.

The best role, though, came in the next, and last, full-scale cabaret. Over the months the Japanese had been steadily sending off groups of Tjihapit prisoners, from hundreds to a few thousand, "on transport" to nobody knew where. Rumours had them ending up in filthy camps in Batavia or on old ships to be torpedoed out at sea. The unexplained relocations scared people: the whispers never stopped that the Japanese really just wanted to kill us all off. By now the upper half of the camp was almost empty. It was said a fence was going to go up through the middle and we in Lower Tjihapit would be herded into Upper Tjihapit. If this were true, *Les deux ânes* would lose its the-atre. So Corry Vonk worked us hard.

By opening night we knew the move to Upper Tjihapit could come any day. The mood in camp was nervous. Change, adults said, was now never for the better. I was already sure that just as my brother had left my life, so would the Crone family, Corry Vonk and Puk Meijer, our room with the window, being an actor, everybody, everything. That's how it went.

Corry Vonk wasn't down, though. The theatre was packed as usual. She looked through the hole in the curtain, then held up a hand with fingers spread, and told us loudly, "Five Japs out front!" She seemed to like danger. The word "Jap" was strictly forbidden because the Japanese had learned it was meant as a slur; if children said it, their mothers were punished; everybody used it anyway, but quietly.

The curtain rose and there in the kitchen chairs, in starched uniforms and gleaming riding boots, swords dangling, sat the commandant and four unknown officers. Corry Vonk was on first and, in her street-boy clothes, gave a short speech she'd memorized in Japanese. The audience was silent, but the military men clapped hard. The commandant had asked her for it especially, to impress his visitors.

Once the show was on the way it moved fast, everyone trying to keep pace with the star who switched from urchin to parlour maid to poet to radish vendor to rabbit to professor. My number was towards the end but I'd wriggled into my tight, hot costume long before curtain time. The skit was about water, which in the sapping heat was always on people's minds. The Japanese pestered and punished us by cutting water off unexpectedly. That was the point of our routine, that never ever could you take water for granted. Two women dressed as pine trees, straight and unmoving, would first hold a long, comical conversation, then drift into a song that ended in a six-line chorus. I would come on during the chorus. Timing was everything. I wasn't nervous, just very ready: the cast had applauded me during dress rehearsal.

When we got to the sketch there was the quick black-out in which the pine trees rushed to centre stage. The lights went on and from the wings I watched the pines talking. There were a few smiles, but no laughs from the audience: to the barefoot women and ragged children, jokes about water or food weren't really funny. The trees went into their song and I bent down, fingertips to the floor. Then the trees sang the first line of the chorus.

"It's grand to be a pine tree,"

And I trotted out on all fours and moved between the trees, tongue out, rear end wagging.

"One of the upper ranks,"

I looked down into the blank faces of the five officers. I sniffed one tree, then the other. There was a chuckle starting, some children pointed.

"Who need but wait and get for free"

The chuckle rose into laughter—as I lifted my leg high to the first tree.

"The special water they deserve, you see!"

Laughter.

"Who need but wait and get for free"

Laughter and applause—as I raised my other leg and "peed" on the second tree.

"The special water they deserve, you see!"

The Japanese below were laughing and clapping, one hitting his thigh.

At the end of the show the cast jogged one by one on stage to applause, and there was, truly, a quick surge for me. But it was nothing compared to the roar that greeted the small woman who, after a moment's pause, and then at a run, came out last. That's who they had been waiting for, those tired, skinny women and children scrambling upright now. For a short while she had held off hunger, fear, and pain, squelched misery, and scattered amongst them like fireflies sparks of her courage and joy. For a long moment then, the audience ignored the five sitting military men, and stomped bare feet, held up children, shouted "Bravo!" and whooped and clapped and whistled. "You're wonderful," she mouthed, eyes wet, "you are wonderful."

ELEVEN / Zuseke Crone

IF THE FIRST HERO looked like a toy, the second, Mrs Crone, was like a tree. She wrote the poem on shitting and was the mother of Ankie, Greddie, and now long-gone Harry. Tall and lean, she had a bony face with the family's slanted eyes, and thick black hair; all her parts were big. Soon after we moved into Tjihapit, she and my mother became good friends. My mother had few friends, although she liked everybody—no, that's wrong: what she did, as she often enough said I should do, was "take people as they are, enjoy the good and forget the bad" and "mind your own business." This was smart because, through all the camps, she never once had a fight, not even a real argument. Anyway, she was friends with Mrs Crone so I trusted Mrs Crone.

Even long after Mrs Crone wasn't in our lives any more, my mother would say that she was the most "forthright" person she'd ever met; and I overheard Mrs Crone call my mother "exceptional." But Mrs Crone wasn't "a figure who remains in the shadow" and she did not "forget the bad." She was a fighter, and I never saw her back off or lose. In our house and at her job, she went after bullies, liars, thieves, cheats, slackers, loudmouths, and dirt-makers. She fought with words. She had her sharp poems, and she had at her command a million sayings. Her tongue was as fast as Corry Vonk's, though not as funny, and because she had a saying for everything she usually also had the last word—which, of course, could be irritating. Yet, adults in our house repeated her sayings; it seemed to cheer them up. They said she was "full of truth," but also nicknamed her "Boss Crone." The sayings were old ones from Holland that she called "the daughters of daily experience." Many, to be honest, I didn't understand. I told her this once and she said I shouldn't worry because "In the concert of life no one gets a program."

Mrs Crone was paid attention wherever she happened to be, but she had no "centre" to her life the way Corry Vonk had her cabaret. No one did. Women worked all day in the sun and then trudged home to take care of children or the sick or old, wash and repair clothes, and sleep. They seldom visited. Early on in Bloemenkamp, yes—we'd even had our party—but in Tjihapit they were too tired and, later, too weak. So my mother and Mrs Crone were good friends in passing; they had no real conversations, not like Ankie and I. They chatted in line-ups in the back of the house where the toilet and bathhouse were and by a short, uncovered length of gas pipe. (It was forbidden to cook at home and stoves had been confiscated, but for a while the gas wasn't cut off. Someone, perhaps Willie—he was smart enough—had fixed a piece of hose to the pipe so it fed a secret little burner. Women met there when they had an extra bit of food to fry or boil; if soldiers suddenly appeared, the all-purpose alarm cry sounded, "Coffee is ready!") Otherwise, they stayed mostly in their own rooms. At one point my mother was taken out of the camp kitchen and made a furniture lady again, on the same team as Mrs Crone. But they wouldn't have talked much hauling the big carts around.

"A friend at your back is like a firm bridge," was a Mrs Crone saying. When Harry was taken away, my mother stood next to her waving goodbye. And later, when Jerry was trucked out of camp, Mrs Crone put her arm around my mother. One day my mother turned yellow, copper yellow, even the whites of her eyes; her forehead burned, and she was suddenly so weak she could hardly speak. She had yellow fever, jaundice. Except to bathe her with wet cloths, Jerry and I hadn't known what to do. I'd never seen her ill and I wouldn't again in the camps; she wouldn't "allow" it. I once watched her late at night in her white cotton nightgown, hair falling over her face, drag herself out of our room on hands and knees, down the hall, and outside to the toilet. I didn't help her because I was sure she'd waited until she thought we were asleep to be private.

The only foods she apparently should and could take in were yoghurt and buttermilk. Mrs Crone found some. I wanted to hear how, but you never asked: it was better not to know. And it was Mrs Crone who every morning would half-carry my mother to wherever their team gathered because the movers' payment of an extra chunk of bread was only handed out to the worker herself. Mrs Crone would hide my mother in an already emptied house nearby, where she lay on the floor until the bread was delivered. Then Mrs Crone would fetch her, prop her up in the breadline, and later sneak away to help her home again. The reason for all this effort was that I didn't get extra bread like Jerry, who also earned it at his job, because I was too young to work. My mother had always split this ration with me and she wasn't going to let me go without. Mrs Crone dragged my mother around the whole two weeks she was sick.

I thought Mrs Crone's face should be carved in stone. With her hollow, lined cheeks, high forehead, and sharp nose, she looked like a hawk. Or maybe a painting would be better.

Because how, in stone, could you cut a twinkle or a glare? You could read the eyes of the animals Hanneke Staal drew. And it was the expression in Mrs Crone's eyes that told me how she meant a saying, as a joke or a swipe, even if its sense went over my head. She was a hero I didn't understand very well but that was all right. Her phrases rolled and echoed around in my mind:

That helps as much as a mosquito peeing in the Rhine.

She's like a winter's day: quick and dirty.

Old love doesn't rust.

Whores and crooks are always talking about honour.

Revenge is honey in the mouth but poison in the heart.

What gain is there if a lazy wench for once rises early?

I know my way around there like a herring in a hayloft.

Quick is dead but Slow is still alive.

Grief is a long death; death is a short grief.

A cow quickly forgets she was a calf.

Don't hoist old horses out of the canal.

Hunger eats through stone walls.

When children are small they step on your toes, but when they grow up they step on your heart.

Young and old, in the end all turn cold.

A warm bed and lazy ass are like lovers: they don't part easily.

Better to have ridden a good horse for half a year, than a donkey your whole life.

Avarice is never satiated until the mouth is full of earth.

Good is good, but better is better.

All things are possible except biting off your own nose.

She's as comfortable as a salmon on a pyramid.

Mrs Crone had two favourites: "Be trustworthy, but trust no one" and "That (some annoyance) is unimportant in the drama of the here and now."

I couldn't, as with Ankie, have serious talks with Mrs Crone: she had no patience discussing death, fear, guilt, and certainly not Manang's spirits; for that sort of thing she had all the answers. But she liked reports. She listened to the killing of Leo the dog, burying the boar's head, food line-up gossip, cabaret adventures, and anything on the horrid Mrs Slierendrecht. They were enemies: "Mrs Slierendrecht," said Mrs Crone, "crept out of hell while the devil was sleeping."

If I had news, I felt free to knock on her door. The room was neat as I imagined Mr Crone's cabin was on his ship, but, as Ankie had said, not *gezellig* like ours. Sitting on their one chair, Mrs Crone might suddenly pull me onto her huge lap, her arms sticky from the heat. "A good listener needs only half a word," she'd told me once, so I'd keep the report short, jump down, and leave.

Then came the morning they took Jerry away, and for a few days I kept to myself. At night my mother and I talked about him, his smell and shadow not gone yet. I was surprised, after my father, Manang, Mrs Plomp, and all the others, how much missing a person could still hurt. Closing my eyes so only a glimmer of light slipped in I thought I could see his face. But I knew that, really, like everybody else, Jerry was fading into mist.

During one of those days, returning from the toilet, I passed Mrs Crone's door and she called me to come in. She was alone, sitting on her chair. In her quick way she yanked me onto her lap. She had been thinking, she said, and she needed to tell me something privately.

"You and I are friends, aren't we?" she asked, her glinting, slanted eyes looking into mine.

I nodded.

"True true friends?"

I nodded again.

"Ernest, a true friend doesn't call me Mrs Crone. He doesn't call me aunt. He calls me—from now on—Zuseke. All right?"

And then the toughest woman in the house, maybe in the whole camp, gave me a sweaty hug.

I was flabbergasted. It was unheard of. Even Dutch adults usually used first names only with family or good friends; in camp many women still said Mrs to each other. For a child to speak like that—like a grown-up—to a woman with children, to a woman who always won, to a woman who should be carved in stone, well, it was hard to believe. It was like a present, maybe as big as Jerry's bike. I was very pleased.

Mrs Crone set me down. Then she shook my hand.

"Sleep well, Ernest," she said.

"Sleep well … Zuseke," I said.

For the first few days after that I tore around looking for her so I could call out, "Hello, Zuseke!" even if I'd just seen her. Others in the house looked up surprised—most of them couldn't be that familiar with her. Was I being cocky? But who got cocky with Mrs Crone? Ankie and Greddie had to get used to it. I never completely got used to it myself.

Time drifted on. But it often felt as if it wasn't real time, as if we were all standing still. The events and people that would stir me were like little flames that camp life quickly dimmed, or smothered. One morning, coming out of a sewer alley, I saw a boy run by chewing a piece of sugar cane. I chased him, but he disappeared. I could *taste* the sugar cane. I criss-crossed the camp looking for him: maybe he had more, to swap, or he'd at least tell me where he got it. As the sun climbed, its heat softened the surface of streets so that bubbles formed; some would burst, leaking drops of shiny black asphalt that stuck to my feet. Hours later I sat down, feeling dizzy. I'd also forgotten what I was doing on the other side of the camp.

It was the same, in a way, when for a few days men prisoners came in to put up the bamboo fence cutting Tjihapit in two. It was exciting at first to see white men after seeing none for two years or more, and guards were posted to keep us apart. The Japanese soldiers, though, faced the women because it was women who risked and got beatings, pressing close and shouting the names of husbands and sons; the men hardly responded and, backs turned, obediently stuck to the job. Their clothes were shabbier than ours—maybe they didn't know how to patch and wash them, or maybe they didn't care. Most of them shuffled about, round-shouldered, heads down—even though women and children were watching. Zuseke mockingly called them "the bruised ones" or "bruisies." I thought they just looked sorry for themselves, not the way men should, and after the second day didn't bother going to the work site any more.

The rumours of moving to Upper Tjihapit turned urgent. Three performances of the last cabaret had been held when, with less than a day's warning, we were ordered to show up by number at the gate in the new fence. As usual we could bring what we could carry; once again sidewalks were piled with tagged mattresses to be carted away. Relocation would take two days. Our house emptied on the first morning, except for my mother and me because we had higher numbers.

Lifting one of their suitcases on my head, I said I'd see the Crones through inspection. That earned an Ankie smile, as I knew it would, and pleased Zuseke, who said, "The bad get worse here, the good better." There was a line-up at the gate, of course, and each foot forward seemed to take an hour. Finicky guards dug through every piece of baggage while the owners stood bowed; there were no tables, and bags, trunks, and baskets were spread out on the street. To possess anything forbidden had become almost as bad a crime as *gedekken.* In the murmuring crowd behind us a retarded boy stared at a hard turd in his fist. Why did his mother let him? His mother had grey straggly hair; two little girls clutched her legs and she looked ahead shielding her eyes with her hands. She went on standing like that.

Finally, in early afternoon, when the sun was pure white, Zuseke, Ankie, Greddie, and I reached the soldiers. We quickly opened the suitcases, took a step back, and bowed, feet together. A soldier named Tesuka bent and rummaged through the cases, spilling contents on the asphalt. At the bottom of the last and biggest one he flicked open a little cloth-covered jewel box. It held a tangle of girl things of Ankie's and Greddie's: ribbons, hairpins, bits of cloth, a lipstick, a necklace, dried flowers, spools of thread. Tesuka bent deeper, plucked inside it. Then, with a grunt, he fished out a small photograph of Mr Crone in his captain's uniform—I heard Ankie sucking in her breath— and after more fingering, a silver Dutch ten-cent piece as big as a shirt button.

Tesuka grunted again, his face showing nothing. He kicked the suitcase shut, stepped over it, and yelled something in Japanese at Zuseke, thrusting with his right hand the picture and coin under her bowed face. She shook her head no. It was suddenly silent around us. He yelled something else, and I thought one of the words was *andjing,* Indonesian for "dog." Again Zuseke shook no. Then Tesuka slapped her face, snorting with the effort, and the things in his hand fell to the street. He slapped her again, so hard that big as she was she staggered. But just the once: she parted her feet for a better grip. He beat her several times with his left hand. Each time flesh struck flesh he snorted. But he favoured his right, hitting then swinging back with the nail-side. That hand just streaked back and forth, landing all over Zuseke's face. With each blow sweat sprayed, her hair jumped, blood drops flew from her nose, but her body and her head hardly moved. Tesuka was sweating, too. And then, just as the beating had begun to take on a rhythm, Zuseke slowly came out of her bow and straightened to her full height. Head up, chest out, she towered over him. Tesuka kept on hitting, but he was off balance reaching up. Snarling, he grabbed her arm jerking her forward, stood on the big suitcase, and started again. But something was wrong. The slaps had less force. Hundreds of eyes had seen the big woman rise up and a soldier of the Japanese Imperial Army have to climb on luggage to reach her. Or maybe Tesuka was tired and knew he still had work ahead in the sun. He stopped hitting, stepped off the suitcase, and mopping his face clumped over to another family of prisoners.

Zuseke sagged through her knees and toppled over. Ankie and Greddie, both crying, stretched her out with rolled-up dresses under her head. Two women wetted cloths from water bottles and wiped her bloody face, dribbled water on the swelling welts and bruises, on her chest, on her arms. More women leaned over her with water. That's what she needed, to be cooled off. She lay unmoving, eyes closed, breathing deeply. On my hands and knees beside her, I blew into her hair. The pounding hadn't shaken me up: I'd seen worse. I felt no pity, just pride.

"You're wonderful, Zuseke," I whispered.

She didn't respond. Near her head still lying on the street was the crumpled picture of Mr Crone. I picked it up and slipped it into her still hand. Her lifelessness made me nervous.

"Zuseke," I whispered again, "what would Mr Crone say if he ever met Tesuka?"

Her eyes flew open. She lifted her head. Her daughters and the women hovering around at once began telling her to lie back. Instead, she half sat up.

"Say?" she croaked through thick, cut lips. "What would my husband *say*? 'Here's my hand,' he'd tell that Jap, 'You did what I haven't managed to do in twenty years.'"

Ankie and Greddie and the women around us giggled and laughed. I was shocked. A few minutes later, the Crones gathered their luggage, Zuseke still unsteady, and walked through the gate and out of sight.

The next morning my mother and I moved into Upper Tjihapit, our third camp.

TWELVE / Upper Tjihapit

IN UPPER TJIHAPIT we were allocated a windowless kitchen that was as dark as but even smaller than the storeroom we had had in Bloemenkamp. It was at the back of the house, next to the toilet; the line-up formed outside our door. The room had a built-in counter entirely covered with blue-and-white tiles that showed windmills, sailing boats, and skaters wearing muffs; the walls were speckled with black-green moisture patches. Two mattresses lying flat couldn't fit on the floor, so mine curled up against the tiles. The house was smaller than the one in Lower Tjihapit and more crowded. We had thought the Japanese couldn't shrink space and privacy more, but, as we'd discover soon again, they certainly could. We knew no one in the house.

Earlier that day we had come through the new gate without trouble, except that the guard who searched our two small suitcases and rucksacks tossed away the exercise book in which my mother had copied *The Hermit*. She knew, of course, that anything to do with reading or writing was forbidden, but she'd brought it anyway hoping the Japanese might be less strict on the second moving day. She was wrong: our soldier was as fussy as Tesuka had been with the Crones. The soldier didn't hit her because she'd placed the book at the top of her backpack, unhidden. She didn't read again in camp.

That first evening in Upper Tjihapit as we sat on our mat-tresses talking the day through, my mother told me what had happened the night before and how frightened she had been. Just the two of us had been left in the house in Lower Tjihapit, it was late, and I had fallen asleep after describing in detail Zuseke's beating and braveness. My mother was reading *The Hermit* for the sixth time, knowing she might lose it the next day, when she heard soldiers suddenly slamming into the house. She quickly shut off her light under the black cloth. They flung open doors to empty rooms, thumped their rifle butts, barked at each other. They rattled our door, but it was locked. My mother lay stiff, not breathing; if they kept at it she'd have to open. She wasn't afraid of the Japanese—our high camp num-bers would explain why we were still there—but of how I might react to being jerked awake by shining flashlights and yelling. She was, she said, very scared that, groggy and with Zuseke fresh in mind, I might do "something crazy." I was only about nine but big for my age, and in the dark and confusion the sol-diers could hurt me badly before realizing I was a child. What she hadn't thought through was that the moment they did realize it, of course, they would pitch me aside, and go after her. The soldiers joggled the doorknob once more, then stamped away; I slept on.

I was pleased that my own mother could think I had the nerve to attack two of the enemy no less. What struck me more, though, was that she'd actually been frightened. I'd never known her to be afraid. She was, I thought, like a jujitsu fighter. From watching the Indo boys, and from having been their mark, I knew the trick with jujitsu was to flow with the other's swing, or kick or chop, help it along even, so a lot of power just walloped air, and again and again the attacker lost his balance. My mother seemed to live like that, yielding but springy, like rubber. She didn't get hit. She was cautious and patient, broke few rules, accepted people and situations as they were—but not from fear. It was always "using my common sense," which, in turn, was somehow linked to her other rule, the big one, endlessly repeated to me, "try to be true to yourself" which, really, meant your "best" self: a long list of dos and don'ts that came down to being just plain good. If you were that, she said, well, then, you'd be all right. It seemed to work for her. I asked often enough, "Did that scare you?" "Were you afraid then?" The answer was always no, and she didn't lie.

My mother was made a furniture lady yet again, and I was on my own. Sameness was at its worst in Upper Tjihapit; later, in the fourth and last camp, monotony eased up because heat and hunger and dying got so bad. The Crones lived in Upper Tjihapit, so did Puk Meijer and Corry Vonk, and Ineke, Hanneke, Erik, and Aunt Ina. I rarely visited though: everyone's daily-life circle grew tighter and tighter—food, work, rest. So, like Jerry and all the others, they began fading away; sometimes, I felt I was passing into mist too—away even from myself. I made no new friends. Sameness flowed on. It was as if I was half-asleep. My eyes felt like glass: I saw only what was close, anything far-off was blurred. I walked with my head down, but not, as before, looking for things to play with, only for what might be edible: snails, unripe fruit, spoiled greens in the camp kitchen's garbage ditch. I would sit in shade in small spaces where people couldn't surprise me and stare down at the red earth between my legs; if an ant came along, I'd watch the ant, let it run up a finger and around my hand. I lay on my mattress in our shadowy room, listened to rain, studied the tiles; outside our half-open door, I could hear the toilet line-up shuffling, murmuring. Willie must have lain like that listening to the wash water gurgling in the ditch outside his door.

In the evenings my mother and I talked. She remembered a sweet moment as a girl when she and her mother had been walking arm-in-arm, shopping in Toronto, Canada, and her mother, who never used endearing names such as "Honey" or "Darling," had suddenly called her "Sister" instead of "Anna." To her first high-school dance she had worn her older sister Ada's new yellow dress with puffed sleeves and not one but two boys, "Red" and Cyril, had walked her home. She believed her father didn't think she was very smart, but one day he'd said, "Anna, at least you know what you want—you want to teach. That's something." The brown eyes were far away for a moment. But her days in the sun were long, she was tired, and she'd start yawning. She would loosen her long red hair, turn on her side and, hands folded between her thighs, fall asleep.

One morning my mother said she wasn't going to work—so no extra bread—because all night an infected wisdom tooth had hurt her. Her cheek bulged. There was a nurse who had the tools to pull teeth. I wanted to come along and watch, but no. When she returned, her face was white and she was spitting blood. She mumbled that the nurse, of course, had had to rip the tooth out without a local anaesthetic. We owned five aspirins—but those were for an "emergency." "I'm not sick," she said tightly. "It'll go away." She sat on her mattress, eyes closed, arms around her shins, rocking and rocking, going inside herself. In a sing-songy voice like Manang's, I told her a few Chinese-girl stories from the old days. In one, the girl pretended she was a horse and foolishly galloped through a field of *alang-alang*, tall sharp-edged grass. She came out looking a bloody mess, with bleeding gashes on her legs and arms and face, blood dribbling into her clothes and red boots. She stuck small leaves on some cuts, but that didn't help; she sucked them, but they bled on. Luckily, there was a river nearby. She took off her clothes, scooped out river clay, smeared it all over, and sat down cross-legged in the sun. All day she sat covered in caked bloody clay. She looked scary, and panthers and boars kept their distance. In the evening she washed herself in the river, with spirits in the trees and water spiders watching, and saw that all the cuts had closed. She never ran through *alang-alang* again. Still clasping her legs, my mother had rolled on her side like a ball and was asleep.

Another day, trucks loaded with Red Cross packages drove into camp. This was some time in late 1944, when cats and dogs had been eaten long ago and it was no use hunting rats any more—with so little to feed off, they had disappeared. The Japanese ordered the bulk of the cargo carted out of sight; what was left was to be distributed among the several thousand prisoners. That called for a special announcement. Out on a field in the sun an officer shouted at the interpreter that while we were *busuk*, "rotten" in Indonesian, *busuk* to the ground—even so, the hearts of the good Japanese had only compassion for us. He told us to keep the camp cleaner, dress neater, wear shoes, and not lick our fingers after eating to avoid dysentery. My mother and I shared a can of Spam with three other people, and we were all counted out ten raisins, four dried figs, one Lucky Strike cigarette, and a postage-stamp-size piece of dark chocolate; my mother at once swapped our cigarettes for twenty raisins. There was another Red Cross shipment in 1945.

Then—suddenly as always—we were told that for the second time the Emperor was permitting us to write a postcard;

he was to do so only once more. All cards, though, had to be in by six that evening, and there was to be no time off from work. Also, we couldn't mention the date, the name of the camp, sicknesses, weight loss, or anything else "negative"; we could only report, in Indonesian, "good" news. There was excitement, anxiety, panic. How, first, to draft the so-important twenty-five "free" words allowed per card? Then, how to say it in Indonesian? And, finally, how to copy that version onto the card in print the authorities could read? Possession of all writing materials, after all, was strictly forbidden, not many people knew Indonesian very well, and there was little time. All day women and children raced around the camp bartering, begging, and lining up for pens, pencils, and scraps of paper from those few who'd dared smuggle them in. Next they ran about for help with translation; it always took more words to say something in Indonesian than in Dutch, and women cried cutting short their messages. We sent ours to my father and could really just let him know we were all right and I was growing. Then came the mad sprint to deliver the cards in time to the administration office. The Japanese were good at fine as well as coarse torment.

One afternoon my mother brought home from a house she'd emptied a framed picture of sunflowers in a vase by a painter named Vincent van Gogh. The print flamed with yellows. "Our own sun," she said, and set it on the blue-and-white-tiled counter against the wall. Another day, she and a woman from her moving team carried in a dainty, carved desk of dark, shiny wood. In the cramped half-dark it stood glowing in a corner, unused, tiny drawers empty. "It's beautiful," my mother explained. Now when I lay down during the day, I had, not only the tiles, but the painting and the desk to stare at. We knew, of course, we couldn't keep these things; we could just live with them for a short time.

Reports of transports had started up again. And soon they were true. Groups of some hundreds of prisoners, according to number, got a day's or a night's warning to pack and report at the camp gate at a certain hour. Again no one knew where they were going. It was whispered that this time the Japanese definitely planned to kill us all—perhaps with machine guns, or by setting fire to churches and schools with us locked inside. And I also heard about the "Borneo Plan"—rumours of which floated until the end: the Japanese would ship the women to the island of Borneo to work in mines for about an ounce of rice a day so they'd quickly starve to death, and scatter the children around Java for Indonesians to raise.

The Crones were among the first to be called up. We went over to say goodbye. We hugged, and Ankie cried, but I didn't see them off to the gate. A few days later it was our turn.

Early in the morning the few hundred of us waiting at the camp gate were counted—twice. The Japanese were poor counters, the officers as well as the soldiers. Maybe arithmetic was taught badly in Japan, for whenever they counted us, they almost always made mistakes, and had to begin over again. Flustered, they could quickly get angry then and start yelling and slapping. We were counted often in the camps to make sure no one had escaped—though where could you hide amongst all the brown-skinned people outside?

Again we were weighted down with worn suitcases, sheets knotted into carry-alls, and rucksacks, with pots, pans, and pails dangling from belts. It was a bright day, not hot yet. I wore khaki shorts and my one shirt with, in the buttoned pocket, my harmonica wrapped in its handkerchief. Walking to the gate my mother told me again and again that, no matter what, we had to stick together, hold hands if necessary, even if it meant dropping baggage.

Once through the gate we were jammed into old buses with the windows painted black. *Lekas! Lekas!* "Hurry! Hurry!" The buses started off, and in minutes stopped again. We were rushed out onto the platform of a deserted little railway station with holes in its roof. There was no train and we slumped against our luggage for two hours. But what I was breathing was free air. There was a world outside the camp. In a circle around us, soldiers leaned on rifles; two officers smoked in the shade of the station house. The tracks glittered until they disappeared under a distant bridge. No Indonesians showed themselves. My mother and I had a small mouthful from the bottle of water she carried in a string bag.

Finally, a short train puffed in and came to a stop hissing. I got excited then. This would be fun. I'd almost forgotten my other train ride when I was four from a mountain depot down to Bandung. Because I'd been good, my father, who had a boil in his nose, had let me come along on the trip to the hospital. But the hospital wanted him to stay a few days, so he phoned home, and I travelled back into the mountains alone that night, up front in the locomotive's dark cabin asking the Indonesian engineer a hundred questions. He had let me pull and push oily levers—so I was really driving the train—and, many times, tug at the knotted cord that set off the steam whistle.

The soldiers shouted and pushed us into a line-up—to be counted again. How could our number have changed? There were mistakes; it took a while. Then, with a lot of *Lekas! Lekas!* we were run aboard the wooden fourth-class coaches with benches along the sides. Planks and bamboo matting covered the few windows. My mother and I were lucky and got seats about midway, but more and more prisoners were pressed into our carriage until the floor space between the benches, too, was packed with luggage and children and women, some standing. Then the doors slammed shut. The temperature inside soared and sweat started running out of my hair. I fumbled for the water bottle, but my mother said softly, "Wait." I could hardly make out her face.

"I'm thirsty," I said.

"I know. Me too."

Except for some small children crying and mothers shushing, it was quiet at first. We were waiting for the train to start—but it didn't. It stood there for another hour, or maybe longer, the midday sun beating down on the roof; a few shafts of light shot into the coach when women parted strands of the bamboo window screening. Then with a wrench the train moved off, squealing and clanging, rocked along for ten minutes, and jarred to a stop again. Word went around we were at Bandung's main station. My mother and I ate a little of the boiled rice she'd brought with a swallow of water. The train didn't move again until mid-afternoon.

Inside the coach, one moment in the thick heat and stink became the next moment and then the next and then the next until they melded into just one unending moment. I couldn't think. Thinking was impossible, so all the people and events that might have helped, didn't. They refused to come into my mind: Manang's spirits, the yellow kite, Ankie's smile. I knew the moment had to end, but then I began to believe that it wouldn't. I would always be in the dark with hot wet bodies pushing into me. I felt I would start screaming and keep on screaming and begin hitting around me and keep on hitting. Was I "crazy"? The feeling was like vomit rising and I had to swallow and swallow to keep it down. Some in the coach didn't swallow and there were outbursts of shrieking and flailing around; there was groaning and sobbing, and mothers whacking children. An argument started and turned into a fight. Fights were usually interesting, but not now. Women yelling with voices that broke; slaps; women shouting to stop it, to shut up, to stay calm. There were more arguments, more fights. My mother sat very still, probably with her eyes closed, touching me only now and then because it was so hot. Near us in the dark a woman fell over, crashing into her neighbours; more women and children fainted. Someone began to sing, about a Dutch admiral who'd sunk the Spanish fleet. Others joined her, but it was hard just to breathe, and the song died. Many times people took up a tune, and stopped again. The stink in the coach was of sweat and fear, and of pee and shit. Just about everybody had stomach trouble. There may have been a toilet hole at the front or back of the carriage, but only for those nearby; the rest of us couldn't move. We did it in our pants. It was a long journey, so everyone must have.

When the train lurched out of the big station, the moaning about thirst had already begun. It would not stop. By then the small supply of water people could carry was gone. My mother had said "Wait" many times, but finally our bottle was empty, too.

In a half-hour the train screeched to a stop again. Those who could spy out said it was a little station on the way to Batavia. They said there was no one about. So it went the rest of the afternoon, the evening, and all that night, halting at tiny, empty depots, hunched together swaying and bumping. No food, no water. After dark the heat lessened slightly for some hours and with it angry voices and crying; not the whimpering about thirst, though. At one of the stations Indonesians had lined up pails and basins of water along the platform; our guards kicked them over. Thirst is much worse than hunger. Like a terrible pain in one place, it shuts out all other feeling.

"I'm thirsty," I whispered.

"I know," my mother whispered back.

"Really thirsty."

"Me too."

"I'm thirsty."

"Yes."

"Very thirsty."

"I know," she sort of hummed.

"But I am thirsty."

"I know you are."

"I've never been this thirsty," I hummed, too.

"No, you haven't."

"I want water."

"Our bottle's empty."

"I want water."

"We don't have any more."

"I'm thirsty."

"I know. We'll have to wait."

"I can't."

"We'll have to."

"I want water."

"We'll get water."

"When?"

"When we arrive."

"Where?"

"We'll see."

"There'll be water?"

"Yes."

"Promise?"

"Yes."

"You promise?"

"I promise."

"There'll be enough?"

"Yes."

"You're sure?"

"Positive."

"Lots?"

"Yes, lots."

As the train clattered through the night down towards the sea, heat returned and with it high humidity. In the moist air you could almost taste our stink. I'd heard adults say that compared to Batavia's wet heat, Bandung was dry and cool. When dawn broke, the lookouts said we were nearing Batavia. The usual three-hour Bandung-Batavia run had taken us about twenty.

The train slowed down, halted with a jerk; after the night of stops and starts, most of us stayed stiff and in place. Another small station. But this time, the watchers reported, guards were running up and down the platform. We could hear them yelling. Fear rose again. Were we there? What now? Mothers shook children awake, yanked at luggage; some people stood up. My mother said, "Let's not rush." Then the doors screaked open and soldiers' heads stuck through grey light and bawled at us to come out. *Lekas! Lekas!* People staggered and slithered across the coach's filthy floor, banging into each other, falling, children howling. *Lekas! Lekas!* Out on the platform we huddled in a warm drizzle, a tired, frightened, smelly group, licking rain from our hands and arms. Soldiers carted several old women and a limp child out of the train and laid them down one next to the other. "Dead," I said. My mother nodded. Some women leaned on others, children held tight to legs and handbags. The guards prodded us into a line-up and started to count—until an officer screamed impatiently and we were rushed off the platform, stumbling, clutching each other, and into canvas-covered military trucks. The still figures and a broken suitcase were left on the platform.

The truck's rear flap was struck down tightly, and we were once again all riding, standing up, through an unknown outside, unseeing in the dark. Our truck drove fast, tires sizzling, honking a lot, so it was probably in the lead. The trip lasted about half an hour. The truck stopped, turned sharply, throwing many off their feet, and backed up a bit. I heard the other trucks roaring up, stopping, turning, and reversing. Our flap was slung open and we could see a few yards away a wide gate made of bamboo poles strung with barbed wire: you could look right through it. On either side, though, rounding away from view, ran the familiar high dense *bilik* wall. Where were we? In the air hung a smell like that in the railroad car. Soldiers yelled at us to come down—*Lekas! Lekas!* Off to the side, a small thin officer, legs in shiny boots wide apart, stood watching us from under his umbrella. Behind him I could see a corner of the wide veranda of a grey stone house and some purple bougainvillaea. Clambering off the truck I kept my eyes on the man because, in a very un-Japanese way, his face showed expression: the small mouth looked as if it was smiling.

Lined up facing the gate, we were counted thoroughly this time. Three tired-looking women in patched-up clothes like ours approached the gate from the inside. They bowed to the soldier who opened it for them, bowed towards the officer.

In a loud, not unkind voice, one of the women, wearing a frayed straw hat with a string under her chin, told us we had arrived at camp Kampung Makasar. She didn't smile; nor did the other two. "Kampung Makasar," she said again, as if the name should have meaning for us. The three of them, she said, were the *kaichós*, "camp leaders" in Japanese. We were tired and sleeping space had been arranged. We would be shown where. We must want to wash and eat and that was arranged also. My mother stood in front of me, her khaki shirt dark from sweat, her skirt stained. Today, said the woman, was *yasumi*, "rest time." Tomorrow, the adults and older children would be told what their jobs were. This was a work camp. She repeated that, too—"This is a work camp." Now we should keep to our line-up and follow.

The three turned and bowed to the officer. The soldier at the gate kicked it open so the taut barbed wire trembled. We shuffled inside.

THIRTEEN / Kampung Makasar

IT WAS NIGHT, and we lay waiting for the sound of the *tokkeh* up in the bamboo rafters. A *tokkeh* is a lizard, with large bulging eyes and four toes on each foot, that eats flies. When it grew dark and there was one in the barrack you waited for it to clear its throat, just like a human being, and go *"tokkeh, tokkeh."* If it *tokkehed* seven times it meant good luck. Kampung Makasar's barracks were risky for flies because, besides *tokkehs* and *tjik-tjaks*, a lot of spiders lived there. By order of the Japanese, a team of women in each barrack spent half a day every month swiping at cobwebs with homemade besoms. But webs were quickly spun again—as dense and bulky as those around the pavilion on the plantation, that dream place. And flies had another worry. Every barrack had to deliver a certain number of dead flies to the administration office—at one point, ten per adult per day; I usually caught my mother's quota. The Japanese also endlessly insisted that our barracks be kept clean and swept, mattresses be aired regularly, and clothes be washed with soap. But the insects that infested mattresses didn't seem to mind the sun and there was of course no soap; people rinsed their few clothes and slapped them a little on the stone floors of the bathing huts. Flies loved the blood in the barracks, the smears of squashed-bug blood that streaked bodies, clothing, mattresses, sheets, mosquito nets, luggage, the *bilik* walls, and the bamboo poles supporting the palm-frond roofs. The crushed bugs smelled like lanced boils.

At eight exactly, every night, the barrack's three light bulbs went out and it was instantly very dark; any show of light afterwards was severely punished. Usually, talk went down to whispers then, and stopped. Adults said sleep was needed for strength for the next day's work in the kitchen, hospital, latrines, or shadeless vegetable gardens with water only at noon. That didn't mean, though, that it grew really quiet. Each of the camp's fourteen barracks built amidst coconut trees—it was a plantation once—held from 200 to 300 women and children, by the end some 3,800 people in a space put up for 800. Sleeping platforms of bamboo slats about six feet deep ran the length of a barrack on either side of a red-earth path; high over the path zigzagged rainy-season wash lines although when it rained, the palm-leaf roofs leaked like sieves. Our mattresses had had to be made smaller because an adult's bed space was just under twenty-four inches, a child's under twenty. So on about forty-four inches my mother and I slept, ate, and kept our clothes, spoons, mugs, and bowls. She and I also had a fork, and our small, lidded tin with four tablespoons of brown sugar we'd saved up; we would have had more but she had bartered three spoons and half a spool of thread for a brassiere sewn from a tea towel. With sheets, old curtains, or clothes hung from string, families walled themselves off from neighbours—but we could still hear each other. In the night there a steady, inescapable rumble of sighing, moaning, snoring, coughing, hawking, burping, farting, retching, teeth grinding, sudden cries, sleep-talking, children whining or sobbing, mothers snapping or shushing, feet shuffling to and from the latrines, and, up above, the creak and swish of low-hanging palm leaves grazing the roof.

It was only just past eight. This evening was different because people talked right on in the dark, even laughed. It was a feast day of some sort, Easter perhaps. My mother was lying next to me under half a bed sheet; I had the other half. It was so hot you didn't really need covering but it kept off the mosquitoes, and tucked between sweaty legs prevented them from sticking together. Even this small space my mother had made *gezellig* with a silk scarf, some of Hanneke's animal drawings pinned to our "walls," and a can with leafy papaya branches. She lay on her back with hands under her head, the half-sheet just reaching her knees. Mine covered me; I could even get my head under it.

In the beginning my mother's job had been to clean latrines, narrow ditches behind the bathing huts into which used bath water drained and trickled to cesspools. She poked clog-ups loose—though during rains flooding was unstoppable; the whole camp turned into a steaming red-mud bog then, dangerous for small children—and she scraped clean the soiled edges of the ditches over which people squatted. Nothing the "latrine ladies" did, though, could lighten the stench in the moist air over Makasar. I had no real job, except some sweeping in and around our half of the barrack, and trotting about yelling that bread or soup or rice were ready at the camp kitchen. Now and then I was sent there to fetch pails of steaming tea, a chore I didn't like because, especially after rain, I could slip and fall. It wasn't the scalding but spilling the tea I feared: not the sort of accident easily forgiven. Later, my mother worked in the vegetable gardens and I, too, put in a few hours with other children my age weeding, watering, hacking at the ground; by then I was the biggest boy in camp.

This morning our holiday had begun, as every day, with the six o'clock *tenko*, "roll-call" in Japanese, when we lined up five deep in front of our barrack; there was another one at six in the afternoon. Ours was one of the first barracks, 4A, near the gate, near the officers' stone house. Usually a low-ranking officer and an interpreter did the rounds, but sometimes it was the commandant himself, Lieutenant Tanaka, the officer with the smile-shaped lips I'd seen on our first day.

Kiotsuke! was shouted and we came to attention, then *Keirei!* and we bowed. Heads down, the women in front counted loud and very fast in Japanese: *Ichi-ni-san-shi-go-roku-shichi* … up to ten; then again up to ten, and on. The barrack *hanchó* reported those too sick to show up, and those who had died. When the totals matched, not often on first count, it was *Norei!* and we could stand upright, then troop off. My mother was the first in our line, me behind her, and seven, *shichi*, was her number. You said it like a sneeze, *Shichiiii!*

One afternoon some weeks before the holiday, with Tanaka taking *tenko*, when it came to *Shichi*, my mother said nothing. Bowed, I could see Tanaka's high boots stop in front of her. Someone coughed in the silence, but she didn't react. Tanaka enjoyed hurting women; I'd seen him; I'd heard the screams in the night from his house. Seconds went by. Maybe ten or twenty. Then she said, *"Shichi!"* and the counting raced on. The boots, though, didn't move: for an awful moment Tanaka's eyes were regarding my mother's bowed head, then he slouched on. Afterwards women crowded around. What had gotten into Anna? Her excuse made no sense. "His boots were so shiny," she said. "I forgot where I was." What had Tanaka been thinking looking down on my mother's head? My mind shut off. I stayed near her, but asked nothing. I'd never before been so scared.

Late that night I slipped out to the bath hut and filled a bottle with water to clean myself, then settled outside over the latrine ditch. I was alone there. The sky was full of stars, though it wasn't good to look at them for too long; they were free. People in *Kempeitai* cells never saw stars. Above me rustled the crowns of palm trees, or it could have been spirits whispering. A few times I had climbed such trees in the deep of the night and twisted loose a young coconut spotted during the day. Dangerous, because patrols were out; if they caught me, they'd find my mother. Barrack roofs shimmered in the arc light of the sentry box on stilts close by the stone house.

Tanaka was greatly feared. I had been looking for a smile on the lips of the most brutal camp officer we'd ever had. It was rumoured that once he had even been reprimanded for his cruelty by his superiors in Batavia. A few months before we came, sixteen women led by a doctor had gone to Tanaka to complain about small bread rations. Tanaka was said to have yelled, "You can all die here. There's room enough in the cemetery." He had ordered the kitchen fires doused, the day's cooking fed to the pigs, food withheld from the whole camp for forty-eight hours, and the sixteen protesters beaten, shaved, and locked up in a bamboo cage for five days. When Tanaka punished in person, women couldn't work for days, so no wages of extra bread or soup, and often they had to be hospitalized. That could have happened that afternoon to my mother—and my mind shut off again. I couldn't finish the thought. The other one, that she might die, I never allowed in at all.

Yet, squatting there over the stinking latrine, I realized that soon after coming to Makasar, I could think about other people dying, anybody really—and that I could finish those thoughts. I could think it about Corry Vonk and Puk Meijer and the Staals, who had landed in camp after us, and about people living beside and across from us in the barrack. I could *see* them dead, and it didn't make me sad: dead was dead. The administration office kept the numbers of deaths secret: they didn't want to scare us. People got sick, went to hospital, then disappeared out the gates on stretchers. It was hard to tell how many died because, with new arrivals from other camps, the barracks stayed packed.

I also discovered, after a while in Makasar, that I could walk down our barrack, gloomy even in daylight, past women and children with broken teeth and bleeding gums, hair growing in tufts like Willie's, faces and stomachs and legs bloated from hunger edema and beriberi, boils as big as ping-pong balls, and oozing tropical ulcers for which they had no bandages, nor clothes nor towels to rip into bandages—and not let myself really *see* them: pain was pain. Just as I could play with other kids, run around, do mischief—but make no friends, on purpose: friends went away. Just as, by then, I could admit to myself that I wasn't especially brave—all I had was my crazy laugh; that I'd never hunted wild boars on the plantation, only pretended to. Just as I could still my mother's voice in my head because I'd learned that her common-sense, be true-to-yourself dos and don'ts always had their opposites and that the choice was mine—and if I did wrong it wasn't so hard to forgive myself. In Upper Tjihapit I had been half-asleep, not in Kampung Makasar. Hunger shrunk bodies here, and fear minds, but they also kept you awake, and you had to be awake to stay alive.

It was quiet at the latrine. Night creatures whirred about, some of them biters. I tried again to imagine what might have happened that afternoon, and again failed. But then—it had to be a spirit's trick—just for a second, there appeared Tanaka's smiling face, down below me in the black filthy ditch where it belonged.

When I crept in next to my mother I was still a bit angry about her behaviour at *tenko*. She didn't wake up. But later she must have, as all of us did nearby, when, suddenly cutting into the barrack's usual night noises and silencing them, a solitary old woman who lived on the berth across from us began in a clear, ringing voice to sing "Ave Maria." She sang the whole hymn. When she was done the only sound for long moments was soft crying here and there.

This Easter holiday was to be made special really only by what the camp office had promised for the evening meal: double rice rations, soup with meat—*babad*, the guts of one of the small, fierce pigs prisoners raised for the Japanese—and half a hard-boiled egg per person. We hadn't had egg for a long time. Sometimes I told my mother that the first thing I wanted when we were free was eggs and cold fruit salad. We discussed the different kinds of fruit we would cut up above a bowl to catch the juice. Eggs we would eat in just a few bites because there would be lots of them. Now when we got an egg she'd take our fork and mash it and we'd eat it slowly. That way, she explained, you got all the goodness.

All day, in the gardens, workers looked forward to the feast meal. The gardens were outside the camp. Under guard, prisoners were marched through the gate, past the grey stone house, and across an asphalt highway that led from Batavia to a town called Buitenzorg (Bogor). The vegetables and fruit fed the women's camps in Batavia as well as ours. In the middle of the garden stood a shed where in hot, still air the pigs were fattening for the Japanese. The sky turned white in the heat of the sun, but water for the women and older girls who worked from early morning until mid-afternoon didn't come until noon, in gasoline cans strung by wire to bamboo poles that women carried on their shoulders.

We boys and young girls wore only shorts, so that even if we had a chance to steal vegetables or a small green papaya, we had no place to hide them; and neither, really, did the women who wore blouses, or brassieres, or tea towels tied across their breasts. I never saw it, but I'd heard that one or two guards sometimes turned their eyes away to let a prisoner gobble up a carrot or a handful of beans. On the return to camp, soldiers watched workers closely for suspicious lumps which, if spotted, nearly always earned a beating. Not all Japanese guards and *heihos* aped their commandant when it came to punishing, but many did. And, although in our earlier camps there had always been a few women who betrayed others to the Japanese for favours, tough Kampung Makasar was full of them. It was a dangerous place to break rules.

After roll-call, we stood in line for bread, soup, and the egg. We ate on our bed, saving the egg for last. My mother's long hair in two braids was wrapped around at the back of her head. When we were done with the bread and had drunk the thin soup out of our half-coconut bowls, she looked at me and said:

"Erik was put in hospital this morning."

The Staals lived a couple of barracks away. Erik was about four then, a quiet, nice boy. I liked him. Sometimes we played, me lying down on my stomach while he sat on my bum "drawing" with a wood chip on my back.

"Dysentery," my mother said.

I was sorry about that. I really was. Little kids who went into camp hospital usually didn't come out again. If Erik died, it would make Aunt Ina and his sisters extremely sad. And me too. Just as I thought of Ineke and Hanneke as sisters, I saw him as a sort of little brother. Right now, though, I wanted my mother to start peeling the egg and mashing it.

"I think," she said, "we should give half our egg to Aunt Ina for Erik. We can do that because we are still strong, and we'll have the other half between us."

I didn't know what to say. My mother never said silly things but this seemed silly. You kept what you had and got what you could. People were eating *larongs*, flying ants, if they could catch them, not to mention fried rat and boiled snake. Give half our egg away? Just like that? It didn't make sense, and she'd said it as if it were a natural thing to do, and as if I were a small child who'd just go along with it. Well, I wasn't talked to like that any more. When had anyone last asked me what I wanted to be when I grew up? I wasn't a kid: I didn't pee, I pissed. You didn't give things away—not food; you traded.

"Erik may die, you know."

I understood that. But Aunt Ina, as far as I knew, never mashed eggs for her children; they just ate theirs in a few bites. Besides, how could half an egg possibly make Erik better? He wasn't a strong boy, and he never got brown in the sun, just red.

"It may not help Erik get better, but we should try…."

She paused.

"I think your brother would say yes."

I slid the palm of my hand up and down the bamboo pole by our bed, one of the poles that held up the roof. It felt cool, smooth, a little oily from being grabbed there so often by us climbing in and out. Fastened higher up was one end of a string that held our rolled-up mosquito net, bloodied and full of holes—my mother was a poor seamstress. There was still light, and down the barrack I could see children curled up already asleep, adults lying down or sitting in their "rooms," as every evening, playing cards, sewing, combing each other's hair, staring, but also chatting which wasn't done much any more. I clamped my teeth tight. I did not want to give in to giving. But it was true, Jerry probably would have said yes.

So, in the end, we put away the half-egg for Aunt Ina ... who probably let Erik just gulp it down.

Our own half she mashed with the fork in one of the licked-clean coconut bowls, then divided it into two neat piles which we ate slowly. Next she gave herself a spoonful of sugar from the tin can and me a spoon and a half because, she said, I was a child and on a feast day children should always be given a bit extra. We ate the sugar slowly too.

In a little while it was eight o'clock and the light bulbs went out. She lay next to me under our mosquito net, and I knew that her hair was not in braids any more but lying loose about her head. Long ago, when I was about Erik's age, she had let me brush it.

People went on talking softly and sometimes laughing, even though they should save their strength. But it didn't go on for very long. I was sure that they, like me, were waiting for the *tokkeh* to clear its throat.

FOURTEEN / Hubie and I

HUBIE VAN BOXEL became my best friend, but I did have to get used to him. He and his mother and two grown-up sisters moved into our barrack a couple of months after my mother and I had settled in. I watched Hubie and the three women put away clothes, bedding, tin mugs, eating pans; his mother strung a pair of riding boots from a rafter above their sleeping space. The women's eyes seemed always to be on Hubie. I would learn later that anything he asked for they gave him, if they had it, or brought to him, like a drink of water. He looked about my age, going on eleven, and my size, which made him the other biggest boy in the camp.

It wasn't just Hubie's family who treated him as if he were special—everybody did. He smiled a lot, which wasn't usual, and he was respectful, which many children weren't any more. I was polite when my mother was around and when it was useful. I roamed Kampung Makasar always with an eye out for "helping" people: fetch, carry, lift, watch a child so its mother could sleep or visit the hospital; if it paid off in a little fee of food, fine, I'd be back. I also drifted around the kitchen and the food sheds, to help, friendly and polite.

I thought, though, that the real reason for the interest in Hubie was probably his hair, which grew in tiny curls tight against his head and was golden. That's the word people used, golden. And because his mother and sisters looked after him so well, so that in the muggy heat he always looked fresh and clean, there was a shine to it, like light. Anyhow, people seemed to enjoy seeing Hubie; the guards, too. I heard some women and girls and even my mother say about him, "He looks like an angel."

On Hubie's first day I hung around his part of the barrack until he had to come over and talk to me. He was wearing only shorts but, whatever camp he'd come from, his mother must have made him wear a shirt because he wasn't very tanned. I was as dark as an Indo boy. His mother's eyes were on us as we wandered away. We sat down on the barrack's shaded side; there wasn't much room because that's where pails, basins, and boxes were stored, washing hung, and a few vegetables and even flowers grown. Maybe Hubie had had to wear a shirt, but I noticed the bottoms of his feet were as hard and full of criss-cross cuts as mine and Manang's. I had no wish to become friends—friends went away—but I knew that we would other-wise have to fight until it became clear which one of us won most often. I was to discover, though, that Hubie, like Jerry, didn't like fighting, not even for fun, so I needn't have made friends at all. But by then it was too late. By then, although it wasn't easy, I had even learned not to mind that people's eyes were always on him.

The smile, politeness, and hair had nothing to do with why we immediately got along. Hubie wanted to know all about Kampung Makasar—food, rules, work, the commandant—and I was the perfect person to tell him. Inmates always snubbed new arrivals at first because they used up space and food supplies, and I knew what it was like to have to poke around on your own. It was a fine, new feeling to be a guide and teacher. Before and after my afternoon shift in the gardens, which Hubie would also take on, I showed him around the camp and explained its workings. Soon he knew the place as well as I did, but I found out he could never know enough. He'd watch women repair a shed roof, dig out wood-eating white-ant colonies, water the hospital's herb garden—and, smiling and polite, pepper them with whys and hows. My trips to the kitchen were strictly to finagle a bite of food, but Hubie would fix his blue eyes on cursing cooks trying to fire wet kindling, then sound them out on baking bread or spicing the vegetable-water soup; often, he'd also walk away with an extra nibble. Everything seemed to interest Hubie, as it had me—once. Then I began to ape him a little and, when we weren't tired, we rambled around camp, both of us asking questions. We were a team. Because we were big, people noticed us and, for the same reason, Indo boys rarely took us on. I had no need for my crazy laugh any more.

It was the "now" that concerned Hubie, this hour, this day. I was the same. We told each other little about people, events, or places from before—they were gone. And the future, well, it was clear to us. Rumours never stopped in camp, switching from bad to good to bad news; lately they were of the good sort. Just as the Japanese had often sunk Allied fleets, so now the Allies repeatedly sank the Japanese fleet. France was free, Hitler was dead, only the Japanese were fighting on. Definitely, they said, the war would end soon. But Hubie and I knew better: the war wouldn't end at all. All of us, we agreed, would always live in camp and die there, one a little faster than the other, but everybody would get their turn. How could we believe anything else? We were forgotten. Hubie and I didn't tell anyone this, especially our mothers: they would have fretted.

On the side of a barrack was scrawled in charcoal, DON'T SPEAK ABOUT FOOD! But everyone did, all the time, as they always had, going on about pre-war meals, recipes, postwar feasts, and, endlessly, about the shrinking fare of the day. It was hunger that did it, clamping the insides of the body, nesting in the mind, and wearing out both. Daily rations by then were, for breakfast, a slice of bread either so hard it had to be softened with water or so doughy it could barely be swallowed, or a cup of thin sago gruel, weak tea or warm water, and a spoonful of sugar when it wasn't held back; in late afternoon a cup of the lowest-grade rice with sometimes a few peanuts or tiny salted fish, and a cup of vegetable-scrap soup; once a week we got a spoon of salt, and occasionally a teaspoon of hot-pepper paste, a banana, a cup of coffee-water. The two meals stilled hunger for about an hour. Hubie and I agreed we wouldn't talk about food, or try not to.

Everybody else seemed outraged when a baby was born in the camp hospital—the father, of course, had to be an enemy soldier; the mother, therefore, a traitor—but Hubie and I agreed this very rare event in camp was marvellous, and climbed on each other's shoulders to peek through a hospital air vent at that new life in Makasar.

We agreed about a lot; many of our thoughts were the same, although mine might have been a little darker than Hubie's. He trusted more, while I remembered Zuseke's "trust no one." Sometimes he'd still give or share; I didn't. He could feel pity; I could, too, but I'd also learned not to *see* the pain and fear and death around all day. And I'm not sure Hubie understood yet about all dos and don'ts having their opposites; though he did know about a few, such as lying, stealing, and at sunset watching freshly bathed women and girls comb their hair.

Like everyone, we tired quickly, had dizzy spells, or suddenly felt shivery; this was from hunger, we knew. Still, Hubie liked playing—more than I did—and I'd go along. The game of *katrik* needed only two sticks, one about two feet long, the other one foot, and two players or more. The person at bat, at a spot marked with a stone, dangled the small stick from an outstretched hand and with the big stick hit it as far as he could. The fielder had to throw the little stick back as near to the rock as possible; the distance between where it landed and the rock was measured with the short stick and the number scratched in the ground; then the batter switched with a fielder. After the players had had, say, eight turns each, the numbers were added and whoever had the lowest total won. *Katrik* involved no running so it didn't wear you out in the sun. Kids might also gather and set up a *tenko* with bowing, counting, and "punishment" that could get a bit rough. Or we'd pretend to line up for food and in cupped hands receive measured portions of sand and bits of leaf. "Hospital" had snippy nurses, groaning, dying patients, and guards coming to haul off "fakers."

I preferred stalking chores-for-food around camp, but Hubie fussed that my "helping" was too much like begging, so we merely roamed, slowly, alert to anything edible. Just as Makasar held many who told on others, so it also teemed with thieves. The Japanese never intervened; they didn't care if we died, never mind being robbed. We simply weren't worth much attention and, aside from punishment and pestering, it was really their indifference that was to blame for many camp conditions. Hubie and I, for part of the day, had the camp to ourselves, except for the old, the young, and the sick. We could have stolen a lot—stuff to swap for food—but we never did:

that was a real "don't." From the Japanese, of course, we swiped at every chance, which wasn't often.

When Hubie visited, my mother was nice to him, and so were Ineke and Hanneke, who had come to live next to us in the barrack; this was after Aunt Ina had somehow arranged permission to take sick Erik to a hospital in Batavia. When I showed up at Hubie's bed space, though, his mother and sisters were cool. His mother had at once found work in the camp office, mine sweated in the gardens. His father was a high-up army officer, mine just an employee on a plantation. Mrs van Boxel held her head high and seldom spoke to anyone, unusual after years of no one caring who you'd been.

Around that time my mother said that I was becoming a big boy and that after work I should bathe separately. A day or so later, Hubie reported he'd been told the same thing. Our mothers, we were sure, had not discussed this. On most days after work, prisoners were permitted to use the bath huts—dark slippery places that held oil drums brimming with water. Dust from the outside garden's red earth mixed with sweat dried into crusts. You dipped a can in and splashed yourself, rubbed at the dirt with a rag, and rinsed again. People laughed in there and yelped. The water falling from arms stretched high made women's bodies glisten. Hubie and I obeyed our mothers and waited until the women and girls were done. While waiting, we'd sometimes go to a hole in the back of the bath hut and stare.

I might have been looking for a Hubie all those years in camp, someone I could feel safe and restful with as I had with Manang. Hubie and I meandered around or lay about in the shade, and half the time we didn't even need to talk. And this was a boy my own age, an equal. Well, not entirely equal: he did have something that, the moment he showed it to me, I envied and immediately and badly wanted for myself. It was a helmetted plaster soldier, probably Belgian—Hubie wasn't sure—in a greatcoat, seated on a horse with a broken tail. It was his one possession, carried from camp to camp. It lit a fierce old longing in me. I dug up my one and only object of value, my harmonica, and pressed Hubie to trade. But no, he liked his soldier. I tried several more times, and he refused; it wasn't as if he ever played with it either.

If after we had bathed and eaten it was still light, Hubie and I might once more circle a few barracks, the office, the hospital, the kitchen, always on the lookout for food, and check the high fence for hidden holes. Sometimes we'd find one, which meant that even though most people had little left to barter and our commandant was so harsh, a few women were still smuggling. When a *gedekker* was caught, always at night, the guard would run her over to the officers' stone house, up the steps onto the veranda. There the usual happened: her hair was cut off with barber's clippers and Tanaka yelled at her and hit and kicked her until he grew tired. Our barrack would grow still then and we could hear every blow. Afterwards she'd be locked in a cage for some days, dependent on brave friends to sneak food and water to her. Some women took these risks to feed themselves and family, some to help the sick, and some to trade the eggs and fruit and sugar for huge profit or services from fellow prisoners.

Hubie and I didn't prowl only in daylight. Sometimes we'd sneak away long after lights-out when it was forbidden to leave the barrack except to use the nearest latrine. We did this knowing that if we were caught we might get a slap, but that our mothers would be severely punished. We'd meet at the latrine, then flit from shadow to shadow through the empty camp to the kitchen. There might be some burnt rice at the bottom of a cooking drum, or a swallow of soup. A food shed might have been left unlocked. One of those sheds was stocked with pig food, hard, brick-sized, soya-bean cakes called *bungkil*. It was mixed with water into swill for the pigs; people could eat it like that, or roasted. A blue line ran through some cakes and this was said to be poisonous to humans. Once or twice we'd found a hunk of *bungkil*; it tasted like sand.

On what was to be our last night run, Hubie and I had found nothing in the drums, and the storage huts were locked—but then we spotted a hole near the ground in the wall of the *bungkil* shed. Hubie reached in and brought out almost half a cake. We broke it into pieces and roasted them in the still-hot ashes of a kitchen fire hole, then climbed onto the slithery palm-leaf roof of the kitchen and sat very still, close together, gnawing at the *bungkil*. We felt it filling us. We felt strong and wanted to laugh and punch each other. We ate it all—there was no thought of sharing with anyone else. In a little while we slid down the roof, sprinted back to the barrack, and lay down beside our sleeping mothers.

Two or three hours later that same night beating sounds and screams welled up from the stone house. They didn't stop until just before the six o'clock roll-call for which the commandant himself came by. Beside him walked the interpreter and behind him, wearing only panties and brassieres, stumbled two trembling young women, each held up by a soldier; their bodies were blotched with welts and black bruises, and smeared with blood, even their bald heads. Tanaka shouted, appearing as always to smile, and the translator told us that he had decided that no prisoner must ever again try to smuggle in food of which he gave us plenty. He had punished the women, as we could see, and now he would punish the whole camp because "your spirit is not good." We must remain inside our barrack for the next two days and we would not be fed. Then the little group moved on.

No one now felt sorry for the two young women, especially after we heard they were *gragas*, "greedy," smugglers. It was rumoured that the Indonesian they had bartered with was beaten to death. It had been a dangerous night for Hubie and me to have taken our run.

People hurriedly carried water in mugs and eating pans into the barracks, lay down on their beds, talked softly, dozed. My mother said we should stay this quiet to save our strength; like most, we had no reserves of food. Hubie and I remained in our own spaces. The two hunger days made many people very ill; some died, older women, patients in hospital, and the woman across from us who'd sung "Ave Maria."

At the *tenko* that ended the punishment, the interpreter read out a harangue by Tanaka. The last words caused great excitement: "You are not stateless, you have a fatherland. Look to the future, conduct yourselves as true patriots, and cast no shame on your country." It could mean only one thing: Holland was free. But why had he told us? Why now? Were the Allies winning against the Japanese? Were they close by? Where?

On the third day, Hubie didn't show up in the gardens. One of the other working children said that during the hunger days she'd seen him being carried to the hospital. I ran there when I got back to camp, but the nurse wouldn't let me in because I wasn't family. Mrs van Boxel and her daughters in the meantime had hung up more sheets around their bed space, curtaining it tightly shut. The next day we heard something that was hard to believe: the Japanese were taking Hubie to their own military hospital in Batavia.

Along with his crying mother and sisters, at least a dozen people were waiting at the camp gate early next morning when Hubie was carried through on a stretcher and lifted into the back of a small truck. He lay curled up, not seeing us, looking about half my size.

The van Boxels stayed behind their sheets. I went to work, and lay on my mattress. Don't die, Hubie. Don't die. Don't let him die, Jesus. Some days passed and then my mother took me for a little walk. She said she had heard that the military doctors had done their very best for Hubie. They had all liked him, she said; anything he wanted they had given him. Apparently he had asked for sliced bananas with milk and brown sugar.

I stood outside the van Boxels' sleeping space that evening and listened to the sobbing. I stayed awake and much later crept near again. It was quiet. Then someone slipped from behind the sheets and moved outside, and I followed. It was Mrs van Boxel wrapped in a big towel with a smaller one over her head. At the latrine I squatted a distance behind her; there must have been stars because I could see the white skin of her shoulders. As soft as a spirit I whispered that I was sorry that Hubie was dead. The head under the towel turned a little and nodded. I asked if she knew we had eaten from the same piece of *bungkil*. She nodded again. Then I heard her whisper that she didn't want to face her husband because, oh, he would be so sad about losing his son.

Time in Makasar speeded up. So many good rumours were flying that people hardly even talked about food. The war was ending, the war was ending—really, this time, really. I learned there was actually a radio hidden in camp, smuggled in by brave women each carrying a tiny part. One evening, it must have been in the second half of August, 1945, the administration office asked us to assemble on a field on the other side of Makasar. I'd once or twice seen Puk Meijer and some girls dance in a corner of the field. It was dark when we got there; even those who could hardly walk had come. I saw no guards. You could have heard a butterfly when one of the camp *kaichós* began to speak. She said she had news but, please, we must not shout or sing. Outside, Indonesians were in rebellion—they wanted Indonesia back. They already knew our news and if they suddenly heard loud cheering they might become angry and there weren't enough soldiers to defend us. When she was done there would be two minutes of silence. Then she said, "The war is over." American pilots had bombed Japan and the Japanese had capitulated. Allied soldiers would land on Java any day now. Until then, camp life should go on as normal, though no working in the gardens, and no more bowing either. Rations would be increased, but food would still have to be cooked and latrines cleaned. Everyone was to stay calm. Three thousand or more women and children were on that field, but the two minutes were very still. A few people cried, but most, like my mother, just stood there, like stones. Hubie had died two weeks before, believing he and I were right, that the war would never end.

A few days later, I was sitting with other kids on the high bamboo fence, barbed wire jabbing our bony bums, screaming and waving at an airplane dropping parachutes on Makasar from which swung big wooden boxes. The plane turned and roared back low, tossing out more boxes. Chocolate, canned food, milk powder, medicine, cigarettes. That on top of the oil, fruit, sugar, soap, toothpaste, and extra rice and bread already distributed in camp.

There was no lights-out any more and that night I watched young women wind up a gramophone from who knows where— in a dimly lit, stone-floored shed, open on three sides, where Corry Vonk had performed a few times. They put on jazz records, and talked and smoked. Word spread and women of all ages began drifting in; many had pinned on their clothes a bit of orange ribbon or cloth for Holland's royal House of Orange. Some wore their "for-when-we're-free" dresses, hoarded for years, but most had on the usual flimsy odds and ends. All, though, looked fresh and clean and combed; there were red lips in the hut and even traces of perfume. One woman shyly put her arms around another and slowly, awkwardly, they started to dance. Other women made room, and a second couple stepped out, and then another, and in moments the stone floor was full of thin and clumsy dancing women. Laughing and tripping, shrieking and pushing, they soon drowned out the music. A few cried and partners hugged them; others smiled like children; some had cigarettes dangling from their mouths; and in the close hot air all sweated, blouses and shirts clinging to their wonderful swellings, breasts small and medium, none big.

Shirtless, and also sweating, I leaned against a bamboo support pole on the edge of the dance floor hedged now by clapping, swaying women. All around me they were smoking; one woman pinched a cigarette in two, offered half, and lit it for me. I felt their eyes, and inhaled, and then exhaled through my nose. "A man," the woman sighed to her friends. I couldn't help myself: slowly I heaved my chest up and gripped the pole so arm muscles would show. "Thank you very much," I said to her, and she grinned and looked into my eyes. I breathed deeply—mystery, mystery—and strolled on to the next pole. "How are you?"

and "Are you happy?" I asked, smiling at complete strangers. At the second pole, a whole cigarette was placed between my lips and lit for me. Then a hand reached out from the dancers, yanked me on the floor, and I was hopping to keep up with a tall twirling woman as old as my mother. Sweat ran down her cheeks and her hands kept slipping off my shoulders. Face turned aside, she just swung around and around, until I was suddenly loose and staggering backwards, cigarette in my mouth, right into a younger, smaller woman. She grabbed me and began to dance quite differently, slowly, holding me against her. It started to rain and those outside jostled to get under the hut's roof. There wasn't room to dance then and women stood pressed together smoking, talking, humming to the music. I moved amongst their moist, warm bodies, smelling them, feeling so fine that my legs were trembling.

My mother was awake when I slid in next to her. It was very late, she murmured, I should have let her know where I was. But she didn't really seem to mind, and said nothing about my smokey breath. After I'd described the night, she whispered only, "Are you a good dancer?"

Next morning I was squatting with my back against the barrack wall by the front door when two young women in shorts approached carrying pails with washing. My eyes moved slowly up their ankles, calves, thighs, and lingered on their breasts as they walked by. And then, out of nowhere, my mother was leaning down in front of me, lips very thin. She hit me open-handed across the face with such force I fell over. "Don't you dare look at girls or women like that," she said, as angry as I'd ever seen her. She glowered down at me a moment longer. We'd had lots more to eat in the last ten days, but it didn't show yet. Her eyes dark and hollow, the sallow skin of her face was stretched so tight it made the bones stick out. She turned and took long steps back into the barrack. I wasn't entirely sure why I'd been slapped, and didn't really want to ask: I would be careful, though, when my mother was around, how I watched girls and women.

For some time even before the end of the war, the Japanese had stopped coming into camp, except for *tenko*. It was thought then that, clean, healthy men themselves, they had begun to dread our filth and disease. Now they hardly appeared at all and, when they did, avoided looking at us—yet at the sight of a Japanese soldier, everything in you still shouted to bow. Tanaka no one saw again. And then one day there were English soldiers in the stone house who turned a radio on full blast. Soon after, a truck drove off carrying our guards, prisoners now, helpless—but in their uniforms, to me, still frightening; it was a fear that would linger in the months to come even when I would see them in gangs under armed guard repairing roads and bridges.

Things were happening so fast. The camp gate was swung wide open, and left so, with a white soldier on duty who whistled to himself. When a group of English officers first marched into Makasar, some women bowed to them, until they were told to stop. The military men criss-crossed the camp, grim and quiet, walking through barracks, with kids following. What did they think of the fleshless women and children with open sores and swollen legs and faces, the rags on wash lines, the spattered bug blood, the smell? The Englishmen tried not to look at the women they stopped to speak to, I noticed, especially not into their faces. Some women sat crying when we came by and didn't lift their heads: already news of dead men-prisoners had begun filtering in. Well, that was to be expected. Adults told each other with great certainty we'd all have died had the camps lasted another six months.

My father walked through the camp gate one afternoon. We'd been told he was coming, and were waiting. I hadn't seen him for three and a half years. He was not a big man. For this day my mother had saved the green dress she'd worn at the Christmas party in Bloemenkamp; I had on my shirt. My father and mother embraced long with closed eyes, patting each other's shoulders. Then he hugged me and said, "I'm your father." I answered, "Yes, sir." We climbed on our bed and he held my mother's hand. She sat looking at his face. Jerry was fine, my father said, waiting in the camp where they'd lived together in Tjimahi, a town near Bandung. Early the next day we were going there by train, he told us. So soon? What about Ineke and Hanneke, I interrupted. It was all right, my mother assured me, they would join Aunt Ina and Erik in Batavia. Except for clothes, we should leave all our stuff behind, my father directed; everything would be provided in Tjimahi. What about our mattresses, sheets, Hanneke's drawings, I asked; I didn't want anyone else to have them. My father gave me a look, but the blue-grey eyes no longer went inside my head. *"Jongetje,* let your mother and me talk," he said in the low tone I also remembered very well. But no one called me *jongetje,* "little boy," any more; old little boy, maybe. I said nothing and went out. My mother remained silent.

Before we left next morning, one of Hubie's sisters came over to our bed space. She said her mother wanted me to have some of his things. She handed me a soft wool cap like Frenchmen wear, the riding boots that had hung from the rafter, and the soldier on horseback. The boots, she told me, her mother had carried all those years so Hubie could wear them to run to his father when he saw him again; they fitted me perfectly. The soldier I wrapped in the yellowed handkerchief I'd had around my harmonica.

It was hard not to cry when I saw Jerry again; for him, too, I thought, when he saw my mother. He wasn't much taller but even more quiet. He had changed and not changed. For about a year and a half he had carried on his own the brunt of our father's "discipline," yet the two of them seemed to get along fine. Jerry was as gentle and generous as I remembered, but I noticed one thing—he'd made a teasing habit of our father's a bit his own. It came down to interrupting another's comment or story, even in mid-sentence, and slightly, cleverly, twisting the words, so that what had been said took on a different meaning and sounded silly; it was done in fun but could stop conversation cold. I didn't like it, nor, I think, did my mother. I wrestled with thoughts about Jerry. Had our father emptied Jerry of himself a little? Still, the four-year age gap between us seemed to have shrunk and he and I played as I hadn't played since he left.

We lived in a house again inside Kamp Tjimahi, in a camp still because it was easier to protect against the Indonesians fighting the Dutch over who owned Indonesia. Jerry and I liked to climb to the ridge of the roof and straddle it. One afternoon we were, as in long-ago days, fighter pilots, arms stretched sideways, weaving and diving, strafing enemy soldiers running below. We had turned and were swooping back when I put my arms down and started to cry. Jerry flew on a moment, looked back, then carefully clambered around me and off the roof. It was real crying, sobbing and coughing—Hubie was so alive in my mind I kept saying his name. Why was he dead? And why, if he was, wasn't I? Jesus, how could Jesus have let him die? After a while Hubie began to fade and I went on with the day.

It happened again, during a meal, and I left the table and sat down on the floor in another room facing the wall. My family let me be. I thought of Hubie certainly as I cried, and of all the others who one way or another had gone into mist.

And one last time—at the start of an evening in that camp that wasn't one but was, when a violinist from Hungary stood on a chair in a field near our house and played for hundreds of men and women and children sitting around him on the ground. It was music that danced on the air, thrilling, free. I put my head down when the thought of Hubie came along, but then I looked up and saw that playing the violin was such hard work that the man's face was actually shining with sweat.

There was long applause when the Hungarian finished and, as he bowed, and people got up still clapping, some with tears in their eyes, and moved towards him, I felt an urge I hadn't had in a long time. It was a strange feeling. I whispered to my mother and she frowned at first, then nodded yes.

I ran home, dug around in my rucksack brought from Makasar, and ran back. The crowd was tight around the violinist, and I had to struggle through it. When I stood in front of him, a short man with curly black hair, I put out my hand with my harmonica in it. He looked at the harmonica and at me for a moment. Then he smiled, took it, dropped it in his shirt pocket, and turned to an adult admirer. I swallowed. It was gone.

Safe in my backpack was Hubie's soldier on horseback, a thing not for giving.

NOTES

MOST OF THE PEOPLE named in *The Way of the Boy* survived the war except for Uncle Fred Staal who died of dysentery working as a prisoner of war on the Burma-Siam railway; I don't know what happened to Manang, Mr Otten, Peter, Dirk, Johnny Tomato, Willie, Tesuka, or Lieutenant Tanaka.

A few months after the war had ended in 1945, my mother took my brother and me to Canada, her homeland, to recuperate— we were the first civilian survivors from the camps to arrive there—while my father remained in Jakarta and worked for the then still-in-power Dutch government. In 1947, we rejoined my father in Jakarta where the revolution for independence, as throughout Indonesia, had been raging since the Japanese capitulated.

In 1968 I lost Hubie van Boxel's soldier on horseback, but it was found and kindly returned to me twenty-three years later.

EPILOGUE / Back on Java

I SAT NEAR THE EDGE OF THE POND and watched for fish jumping; I never saw any, only the widening rings they left behind. The ample pond was stocked with carp and gourami. Monsoon rains had raised the brown water almost level with the lush lawn and shrubs. My wrought-iron chair stood beside the front door of a two-room guest-house overgrown by an orange bougainvillaea. It was light but the sun didn't show yet; ordinary birds had taken over from the noisy creatures of the night. This was the best hour. Once the sun appeared the heat would soon follow—heat that you breathed and tasted and could see dancing in the hazy air.

There was time; by now a routine had evolved. Renni wouldn't come over from the main house with the tray of tea and sliced papaya for another half hour. I had been awake for hours already: tropical nightlife was still disconcerting. In the dark, inside my little house and around it, there was much rustling, whirring, and the odd squeal, and around 4:30 the muezzins' voices calling the faithful to prayer would swell to a great wail.

During the writing of this book, magazine assignments had brought me back to Java after more than forty years. Throughout most of my short stay, I had been moving along in a kind of dream state—every sight and sound and smell set off waves of memories.

Somewhere in the rear of the garden a woman began to sing tonelessly on and on. I watched big red ants marching along a branch of the bougainvillaea up to the roof, one behind the other. This morning I would be leaving Bogor, a town between Jakarta and Bandung (where three of our camps had been located). I was going on a small journey that would take me about ninety miles south into the mountains in search of the tea plantation, difficult of access, which was our home before the war. I had lived on Java from three to the age of fourteen. For me, remembered consciousness began there. I had come home.

I had landed in Jakarta, as most visitors do, and escaped that city's furor quickly. On the way out, I asked my elderly, English-speaking driver to help me inquire whether anything was left of Kampung Makasar, our last camp. We discovered that the village, which had been near the camp and after which the camp had been named, was now an entire city district. Clerks at the municipal office had never heard of a camp, but then none of them looked more than forty. They wanted to help, though, and guided us to the house of Hajji Mohamad Nur, a retired fruit farmer, who had been a village official in the 1940s.

Tall, straight, seventy-five years old, and a chain smoker of Indonesia's clove-spiced cigarettes, Nur waved his big hands around and was inclined to shout though he wasn't deaf. It was a pleasure, though unexpected, he said, to have us in his home. He was called Hajji, I should understand, because he had made the pilgrimage to Mecca. The camp, he said, had been "a bad and secret place"—bamboo barracks surrounded by a high fence in the middle of vegetable gardens. White women and children worked there. Nur thought that his wife, his blind, ninety-year-old mother-in-law, and he himself were probably the only ones left who remembered it. About three quarters of the people in the area had died in those years, first when the Japanese army took away the food the farmers grew and afterwards during the revolution. He pointed at my driver, at me, at himself, clapped his hands, and laughed loudly: "We have survived!"

I didn't know what to say.

And neither did he then, so he showed us around his small stone house. Oil-lamp smoke had blackened the ceilings. We were allowed a glimpse of a room where a window let in the afternoon's hard light on the child-size, nearly bald figure of his mother-in-law sitting on a brass bed facing a wall.

I asked if anyone had ever felt *kasihan*, pity, for those whites.

"Of course!" Nur said. Young men from the village would make their way to the camp after midnight with fruit and other food, to exchange for clothes or jewellery. But sometimes they'd feel such *kasihan* they'd just throw the food over the fence and run home. He shrugged. After the women and children had been evacuated from Makasar, he said, the Allies had filled the barracks for a while with Japanese prisoners. How those fastidious men must have hated it, I thought, living amidst our filth and bugs and deadly germs.

Nur told us the location of Makasar and we drove by. Today it is an army garrison built of stone, but there's still, as then, a lot of barbed wire about. The road running by is wider and busier, but the main gate, through which I'd peered at freedom, is just where it used to be. Nur had said that neighbourhood people are superstitious about that gate: since 1945, a lot of accidents in which someone invariably is killed have happened right in front of it. It's a puzzle because there's no cross-road. "Many people died inside that place," was Nur's explanation, "and their spirits are still there."

It's easy, in Indonesia, to accept the spirit world's mysteries. Certainly it seemed to be the kindly connivance of "silent forces" that was charting my unplanned rambling.

In Canada I had been asked to deliver a package to Renni Samsoedin in Bogar. I found her to be an immensely cheerful woman in her early thirties with degrees in botany and chemistry. She spoke fluent English and promptly asked why I was in her country. I said I was seeing some places where I'd lived as a boy; now I hoped to seek out the tea plantation. Renni nodded and smiled and nodded. When you talk to Indonesians, it seems sometimes as if part of their consciousness is elsewhere, as if they are dreaming and yet awake.

"Ah well," Renni interrupted, "we must make a plan. You must come and stay where I live—there's lots of room. You will meet my father. He will help with the plan."

Renni was intrigued by the idea of someone returning to where he'd been small—and in *her* Indonesia. It would not do to muddle on alone, though, and try to find the plantation. Just rent a car and go? It wasn't that simple. Or maybe it was, but it was no fun. Or at least it was more fun if Indonesians came along to explain things. Her whole family would help make a plan. There were three girls and seven boys, all adults; Cucu, the youngest, was twenty-two.

Would I return to her office in late afternoon when Cucu picked her up in the family Land Rover—and would I like *saté ayam* (chicken roasted on bamboo skewers in spicy peanut sauce) with *nasi goreng* (fried rice) for dinner?

The rest of the day I explored Kebon Raya, the city's world-famous botanical garden, with its rolling lawns, holy banyan trees, cactus gardens, lily ponds, and forest groves. It was green and still. Left unharmed by the war, it had probably been as green and still while we were in camp. Upside down from the branches of a dead-looking tree hung bats with bodies the size of rats. Now and then one would wake up with a sad cry, spread its cloaklike wings, float to another branch, and fold up again. The huge, many-trunked holy trees possessed massive self-assurance: roots grew down from their branches into the earth, enlarging and renewing the trees forever.

Later at Renni's house the rest of the family wasn't home yet. She first showed me a room where, spread out on the floor, polished and ready, there lay enough flutes, bamboo xylophones, gongs, and other percussion instruments for an entire gamelan ensemble. On Sundays the Samsoedins got together and performed Indonesia's rhythmically complex, liquid, thousand-year-old music for hours on end; but I missed that. Renni walked me around the family's terraced fairytale garden, full of still places, to the little guest-house by the fish pond where I would sleep. I bathed, splashing water over myself in the way I had done so many years ago.

Most of the family came around that evening. Word got out about Renni's foreigner, though none of them had a phone. All knew some English. Pak Samsoedin, the father, also remembered a few words of Dutch. Soft-spoken and much less direct than his daughter, he did eventually ask why I was in Indonesia. Halfway through my reply his attention shifted in that curious Indonesian way.

"So," he said abruptly in English-Dutch, dropping in a word of French as well, "you are going on a journey of *nostalgie?*" He stared ahead. The room was quiet. "I too would like to go on a journey of *nostalgie*. And in the same area. It is beautiful. High in the mountains with the tea…. I was stationed there, you know—in 1947, with the army.

That would have been the revolutionary army fighting us, the Dutch.

"I remember we were put up in a nice house," he went on. "In the morning I would go out and do my exercises on the big downhill lawn…."

He paused, remembering.

I thought I felt some neck hairs rise. I reached for my camera bag and groped inside for a half-dozen tiny black-and-white pictures taken before the war.

"And then I would walk to the edge of the lawn to a bridge over a little stream…."

I held out a photo.

"This house?"

He looked.

"That house, yes."

It was a picture of *our* house on *our* plantation. We'd been trucked away in 1942. The population of Java is more than a *hundred million* . . . ? and *forty-seven years later* . . . ! The family was amused but not awestruck: these things happen. Manang would have understood. Renni laughed and said, "Magic!" Her father took it entirely in stride and continued to reminisce about his army days. But yes, the journey of *nostalgie*. . . .

Cucu would drive me, Cucu was on a break from law school and had time. In a corner on the floor with his seven-year-old niece Dini in his lap, Cucu nodded sleepily. Short and slight, he rarely spoke and always looked sleepy. Renni said that if I could wait a day, she'd take time off and come as interpreter.

Absolutely. The map was spread out on the floor, a jug of chilled coconut juice did the rounds, a route was plotted. The "silent forces" were at it all right. There was a great honking of frogs in the fish pond.

And so, after tea and papaya, we were driving out of Bogor, Cucu at the wheel, Renni in the back. The road at once started to ascend and the air grew drier and clearer. Every day there had been the season's sudden rain squalls, but this day it stayed dry and mostly sunny, allowing the views along the twisting, climbing roads to come spectacularly into their own. Early on, patches of mist had raced over the valleys, over the tender green, terraced rice fields. Where the hillsides carried cuts or stood too steep to cultivate there was unruly jungle growth from which poked the familiar heads of coconut trees. Later, high up where the tea plantings began, the terrain acquired the long sweep of mid-ocean waves: the flat-topped, black-green bushes fell and rose in patterned clusters against red earth from the shadows of one mountain into those of the next. Renni called the weather "magic," as she labelled almost everything slightly fortuitous. But she was right. At a certain point the narrow asphalt roads turned into roads of rock and earth—we'd gone wrong. Had it rained, even the Land Rover might have bogged down.

We were quite alone by then, except for the occasional clutch of women tea pickers in their conical hats, chest-deep among the bushes, hands quick as sparrows pinching off the pale green youngest leaves. The car jolted along in first gear for what seemed hours, but the windows were open and the sun was gentle. A stop for pictures let the uplands' immense still-ness settle for a moment.

We were getting closer to Pasirnanka, the plantation, and my mind was moving awfully fast. We turned a corner and were suddenly amidst houses and people—some of them in dark-blue uniforms, gesticulating at us with night sticks! Security guards yelling, What were we doing here? Who were we? They were clearly astonished to see us: we had come in the back way. How had we known the bridge on the main road had collapsed yesterday. Renni murmured, "Magic"—and cheerfully set about explaining. Cucu, unperturbed, passed around cigarettes.

Was this the plantation? Nothing looked familiar, not a house, not the shape of a hill. I wandered away from the car. My mind was slowing down again. By the guard house a road turned left and down towards a large grey metal shed. I could hear a humming that grew louder as I came closer ... the factory! If that was the factory, then up that hill had to be the swimming pool. And to the right, beyond those new houses, the home of the lovely Mrs Plomp. And from way up their hill, Mr and Mrs Plomp had looked down—on us!

I started to run, and the group by the car followed. A few steps only and there was the Plomp house, a dilapidated bungalow on a little rise, not a hill. And there—our house ... the garden still the same shape; buried deep in the rear a wild boar's skull. On those fieldstone steps my father made Jerry and me promise to look after our mother; the last time we came down them, my mother, Jerry, and I were loaded into the back of the truck with the other white mothers and children. But such a little house! The shape unchanged but walls cut into picture windows, the "pavilion" gone.

The others had caught up. The guards were laughing and calling to someone inside the house. A woman in a pink dress came out; a little boy and girl followed and clung to her legs. The woman looked a bit apprehensive and didn't speak. One of the guards urged her to invite me inside, which she did with her hand. But I said thank you, no, because I knew right then that I had no need to enter, and no curiosity. I took some pictures, thanked her, and started down the steps, the group following. There were quite a few new homes, but those the whites had lived in were still in use too. The biggest had been the chief administrator's, Mr Witte's; his home was in even worse shape than the Plomp place.

Friends and guards in tow, I now marched towards the pool on the hill. At the bottom of the slope there was a tall vine-covered wire fence, broken and flattened in places, the gate hanging open. I knew for certain that there had been no fence there in our time. Inside, high wild grass ran up the hill. I reached the edge of the pool. One rusted handrail still stood upright by the steps leading down; weeds sprouted from the cracked concrete. The guards looked around with interest. The hilltop was quiet, shadowy, neglected—where once it had resounded with life. It was like an old cemetery.

A half-hour out of the plantation, on the way back, Cucu drove off the narrow road to let a small bus pass. He cut the motor and lit a cigarette. As the noise of the bus receded, stillness set in again. Cucu had hardly spoken on the whole trip. He listened to what others said and responded with his eyes or his smile. But then he turned to me sitting next to him and unexpectedly asked, "Are you happy now?"

I thought of the place we had just left and that I'd travelled so far to visit, and I said: "I am, yes"—and realized I was already seeing it again, in my mind's eye, as I'd always seen it, and probably always would. Memory is, finally, all we own.

ACKNOWLEDGMENTS

Thank you to:

Marta Tomins for every day and every page, for providing serenity and the finest editorial skill I know; Maia Hillen for patience and inspiration—in the time it took to write this book, she wrote *and* illustrated half a dozen.

Jerry Hillen, John Hillen, Ankie Sonius-Crone, Zuseke Crone, Hanneke Staal, and Ineke Staal-Wondergem for sharing memory.

Jan Whitford of the Lucinda Vardey Agency for good counsel and care.

Cynthia Good, Publisher of Penguin Books Canada, for understanding and editorial guidance; Mary Adachi for meticulous copy editing.

John Fraser, Editor of *Saturday Night* magazine, for encouragement and for providing a "home" at *SN*; Dianne de Gayardon de Fenoyl and Dianna Symonds for enthusiasm and early reading of the MS; Barbara Moon for abiding interest; Hibo Abdalla and Karen Norell for first-rate printing labours; everyone at *SN* for their good will.

Ian Brown, Danielle Crittenden, Kildare Dobbs, George Galt, William Lowther, Candida van Rees Vellinga, and Peter Worthington for their support.

ACKNOWLEDGMENTS

Rita Davidson, William Davidson, Anita Tomins, and Thomas Eva for forgiving absences.

Mezciems for peace and beauty.

The Toronto Arts Council and the Ontario Arts Council for writing grants.

Segments of this book have appeared in *Saturday Night, The Idler, The Wall Street Journal,* and *Weekend Magazine.*